PRAISE FOR

Doing Business *With Ease* Overseas

"As a financial planner, I need to be able to relate to individuals on a personal and connected level. I have to be able to do this quickly and continuously to ensure that my clients can relate to my recommendations and advice. Mrs. Russell's insights into connecting with people, no matter the differences in culture, have been invaluable to my team for years. *Doing Business With Ease Overseas* will help us to connect more quickly and effectively with clients and prospects by understanding how to best relate to people regardless of their background or culture."

AARON M. VAUGHN, CFP, J.D., AMERIPRISE FINANCIAL

"As publisher of *IndustryWeek* and an executive at Penton Media, one of the largest business media companies in the US, I asked Harriet to help Penton's editors better understand how U.S. manufacturing executives can build more effective cross-cultural relationships. Her seminar was outstanding.

"I'm very impressed! *Doing Business With Ease Overseas* has great value. It's not just another guide to doing business internationally; it provides a comprehensive strategic insight into how business executives need to think to succeed globally, and how vital it is to immerse themselves with cultural natives. Very well organized and written, its easy-to-read format makes this book in my view a must-read for internationally-minded business leaders."

CARL MARINO, (FORMER) PUBLISHER OF *INDUSTRYWEEK*, THE LEADING MANAGEMENT MAGAZINE FOR GLOBAL MANUFACTURING

"Harriet is a wonderful speaker who is always engaging. In this book, as well, she is able to draw the audience in through her use of personal experiences. Harriet shows how it is important to always be aware to be culturally sensitive when dealing with an international audience and when doing business. *Doing Business With Ease Overseas* is a great resource and Harriet is *the* cross-cultural expert to have on your team!"

LISA PURDY, PRESIDENT & CEO, COUNCIL OF INTERNATIONAL PROGRAMS USA

"Harriet Russell's extensive intercultural experience provides a framework for professionals who are preparing to work or visit abroad or who work within a multicultural team in the U.S. She shares examples and lessons learned from her own journey to countries around the world. Harriet will inspire you to become more open, inclusive, and respectful when working in other cultures."

CHRISTINE ZUST, SPEAKER AND AUTHOR OF *EVERYTHING I DO POSITIONS ME: THE SIMPLE PATH TO PROFESSIONAL SUCCESS*

"A fascinating. multi-dimensional approach for interacting with other cultures. This book is an invaluable guide to understanding the dos and don'ts when developing new cultural relationships, whether business, personal, or for anyone just traveling the world. This material is easy to read and includes great examples of life situations for easier understanding.

"Recommended for anyone who wants to develop cross-cultural relationships with more comfort, less stress and an open heart."

DONNA CLAIBORNE, FLIGHT ATTENDANT, UNITED AIRLINES

"I enjoyed this book and you will too. Harriet is a powerful communicator on many levels. She captivates and engages the audience with her intelligence and humor.

"Harriet is a very special soul and teaches from the heart. Her ability to listen, teach, and innately know what is required for understanding is magnificent."

LISA CHAPPELL, NETWORK TECHNOLOGY CONSULTANT, HEWLETT PACKARD

"This practical, engagingly-written book will help anyone doing business with another country or culture, and it will also help travelers who want to interact with locals. Russell's broad experience has opened her heart and her mind, and she shares what she has learned with the reader."

JUDITH FEIN, AWARD-WINNING AUTHOR OF *LIFE IS A TRIP*, TRAVEL JOURNALIST

"A must-read for global business travels. Harriet has the capacity to address issues of the head and the heart. Global connections will benefit greatly from the reader taking both these components into consideration. A thought-provoking look into the differences and similarities between people."

KLEYTON YOUNG, REGIONAL DIRECTOR, METLIFE

"Harriet Russell is charismatic, friendly, energetic and involved. This shows up in her book. Harriet is knowledgeable as well as street-wise. Her wealth of international business know-how, cross-cultural expertise, in-depth information and years of experience in the global realm comes through in *Doing Business With Ease Overseas*. She knows how to salvage a situation, even turn it to her advantage.

"Her idealism and altruism are well balanced with feet-on-the ground realism. An invaluable asset—one such person, one such book, can set the tone for a whole team or group of people working together, in the US or abroad."

MARINA KURKOV, RUSSIAN PROFESSOR

"In your hands, you hold a guide to making positive connections with people from around the world, whether here or abroad. Harriet Russell provides you with what you need to know and do, as well as not do, in order to communicate with respect, honor, and trust.

"Keep this book within reach at all times, refer to it often, and you will build relationships that last a lifetime."

MARK LEBLANC, AUTHOR OF *NEVER BE THE SAME* AND *GROWING YOUR BUSINESS!*

"I am extremely excited about Harriet Russell's latest book, *Doing Business With Ease Overseas: Building Cross-Cultural Relationships That Last.* This book details the essential guidelines for building solid long-term relationships with different cultures. Harriet Russell reminds us that today the world is one family, both at home and abroad."

MARVIN MONTGOMERY (THE SALES DOCTOR), AUTHOR OF *THE PROFESSIONAL GUIDE TO SALES SUCCESS*

"The bottom line is: Harriet gets results and shows you how to in her book. There is no one who is better well-versed in international communication. From customs to body language, Harriet prepares the business person working internationally to hit the ground running."

RICK DUDNICK, VP, LONTOS SALES & MOTIVATION, INC.

"If you plan to grow your business globally, this is a must-read book. It can help you gain a cultural competitive edge and appreciation of what works. A brilliant book by Harriet Russell. Full of practical tips, ideas, and insights from her years of travels, doing global business successfully."

JONATHAN LOW, CSP PCC 2015-16 PRESIDENT, GLOBAL SPEAKERS FEDERATION

"*Doing Business With Ease Overseas* goes beyond theory to provide the actual tools for successful and lasting business relationships with less stress. Harriet Russell takes you further into the root cause of stress and helps you move forward into awareness, understanding, and ease."

LAIGHNE FANNEY, (FORMER) GUEST HOSPITALITY MANAGER, KRIPALU CENTER, AN INTERNATIONAL HOLISTIC YOGA SPA

"In *Doing Business With Ease Overseas*, Harriet Russell has provided an imminently practical primer for navigating new cultures with greater awareness, sensitivity, and ease. There are great gems of wisdom both for business and personal engagement, wherever you may be traveling. In fact, many of Harriet's twenty lessons are even applicable when traveling and working within your own culture. Having worked in more than fifteen countries myself, I wish this book had been available to me ten years ago when I first started working internationally. It would have been very helpful!"

ALAN SEALE, DIRECTOR OF THE CENTER FOR TRANSFORMATIONAL PRESENCE, AUTHOR OF *CREATE A WORLD THAT WORKS*

DEDICATION

This book is dedicated to my Mother, whose unconditional love continues to connect with me beyond time and space.

Her last words to me were:

"Listen.

You are unique.
You are courageous.
You like to be in nature.
You love high adventure.

Be true to yourself."

TABLE OF CONTENTS

SECTION I

A *New Map* for Doing Business

CHARTING THE COURSE

Why the Unease Overseas?

In this book, I take you on an inside view of my personal experiences as a world citizen in business living overseas. I show you how the journey as a world traveler has enriched and enhanced my journey within.

Upon graduating from college in 1974, my only experience abroad was a year in Spain. Then, in 1975, I spent six months traveling overland from Europe through Iran and Afghanistan to India and Nepal. As I followed Marco Polo's Silk Route, I traveled by car, train, and bus. I took the time to immerse myself into the journey.

In each place, I did not know the language, the culture, or the customs. Wherever I went, I was a fish out of water.

I traveled by air to Thailand, the Philippines, and finally to Japan, not knowing Tokyo would be my home for the next five years.

At the start of my career I had education, skills, and some work experience, but I was without a guidebook on what to expect, how to act, or what to say in another culture so distinct from my own. I learned from exposure, experience, and each personal interaction.

As a woman, I learned how to do business successfully without stress through observation, perseverance, and patience.

I understand the unease of overseas. I found shortcuts on how to quickly understand cultures, customs, and etiquette along the way.

Some people like to travel. They are open, courageous, even adventuresome, but also vulnerable.

Some people are afraid to travel. They are cautious about developing meaningful and long-lasting business relationships across the world. They do not know where to begin.

How can we, in this day and age, overcome the fear of the unknown and the discomfort with encountering people who behave, communicate, and live differently? How can we elevate our perspective to make changes?

The best resource is to begin with ourselves. Awareness and attitude make a difference. Do your part. Live authentically, honestly, and positively. Be kind, sincere. Be truthful, especially with yourself. There are two basic emotions: love and fear. All positive emotions are based in love. All negative emotions are based in fear. Will you align with fear or will you align with love?

Companies do not do business; people do business.

The most rewarding cross-cultural understandings are interactions with people.

Surely, I like to see history still alive in the remnants of old architecture, methods of cooking, healing, and handicrafts passed down from generation to generation. The awe-inspiring landscapes and scenery allow me to take a breath and feel alive with reverence for the grandeur of life and Mother Nature.

But it is interactions with people that move me deeply. The connections of the heart. Learning from and accepting differences. The acknowledgment of each individual's specialness and the recognition of our similarities.

You can proceed even though there are difficulties. You can be inspired to act. I hope this book will help you along the way.

In this book I introduce you to cross-cultural business connections by:

- Defining "culture."

- Helping you find ways to categorize behaviors and beliefs of differing cultures and overlay them onto global business.

- Showing you how to move from discomfort and uneasiness to understanding and less stress. We start with our own personal awareness of who we are, how we think, feel and act, and how others perceive us.

- Teaching about others from other cultures.

- Uncovering how to throw away the formulas and learn to trust your own inner guidance and intuition from a calm and peaceful attitude of gratitude and positivity.

THE QUEST:

Cross-Cultural Connections at Home and Abroad

In this global economy and multicultural, multilingual world, bridges are built and crossed. My intent is to help you cross them with ease.

This book is not meant to change your cultural foundation, but to stimulate you into another way of viewing yourself and the world with an expanded consciousness with limitless potential. It can be so rewarding and enriching to learn from other cultures.

The principles of self-awareness, nonjudgment, acceptance of others, and seeing the whole picture are tenets for success in cross-cultural business relations.

I believe that everyone, every action, every thought carries an impact upon this world.

Why not make business life a journey of less stress, open hearts, growth, learning, and development in order to create peaceful as well as profitable business relationships? Cross-cultural competency can do this.

Who Am I?

I lived abroad for eight years in total immersion in my twenties. When I reached thirty, it was as if I had an identity crisis. Was I doing business, interacting, and thinking like an American, a Spaniard, a Japanese, or as Harriet Russell?

I was a blend of all. I had consciously or unconsciously taken in my experiences and adapted them to my persona. I was like a chameleon who changed according to my environment, but I also had a core "me." I observed, adapted, and then integrated into the different cultures.

I came back to the U.S. thinking I needed more real American business experience and education. I started working in New York City at Sony Corporation of America, then the German Metallgesellschaft. Still searching, I went to Bankers Trust on Wall Street to experience what I thought was the all-American style—a U.S. company for a U.S. woman.

For all the external success, I still did not feel at ease. I began a daily practice of meditation. I then took a ten-day program for self-exploration at Kripalu Center for Yoga and Health in Stockbridge, Massachusetts. As soon as I walked in the door, I felt an energy shift. The staff was happy, the attitude was positive, the level of service and professionalism were great, and the scenery and lifestyle just what I wanted.

I began to feel in alignment with who I really was. East meets West, right in Massachusetts. I discovered how moving with ease in life came from within myself.

I went back to New York, left my job, sublet my apartment and returned to Kripalu to live and work for eight years.

For the subsequent thirty years, I have used body-mind stress management techniques and applied them to all areas of my life, including cross-cultural business.

Here are five key points that work for me:

- Positive Attitude

- Trust

- Knowledge

- Patience

- Respect

This book is not intended to cover all the places I have been; neither is it a directory of all the cultures in the world. The personal anecdotes I have selected and shared illustrate points within the framework of the academic field of Intercultural Communications and Business Protocol.

This is my story. And you will have yours. In the sharing of our experiences, we can build lasting business relationships and a stronger, friendlier world.

Letting Go

It is wonderful to know that nothing is wrong or right in cross-cultural differences.

It is just what it is. Different. And the differences in cultures give us possibilities to expand our skill-set toolbox as well as our consciousness.

Rumi, the 13th century poet and Sufi mystic, wrote: "Out beyond ideas of rightdoing and wrongdoing, there is a field. I will meet you there."

An influx of different ways of thinking, acting, perceiving and interacting with the world can be intimidating, even threatening to a person. Yet to another person, it can open our eyes to not only understanding others, but more importantly, to understanding ourselves better.

Cross-cultural awareness begins with asking, "Who am I?"

What values and concepts do we hold? When we are challenged and continue to hold on, we create internal stress. With stress comes negative attitudes, moods, words, and behaviors. Our openness to balanced and healthy inclinations towards kindness, compassion, understanding, and love are blocked.

Holding on does not make you strong. Letting go does.

Relaxing into accepting others as they are releases stress and tension. Just as it takes energy to tense a muscle, it takes energy to hold on to our resistance. When we let go of the tension, we consequently gain energy and can channel it into other areas. We can open our minds and access a heartfelt energy which allows us to move into mental and emotional transformation.

Know yourself. Be yourself. And then explore outside yourself and try new ways. See how they feel. Understand from the inside. Then you can make conscious choices.

Knowledge Is Power

We are always changing. Yet the inner core of who we are, the love and light, is constant. How you find that inner self is personal to each individual. That it exists in everyone is undeniable.

How to break through the layers of differences to find the connections of similarity is what cross-cultural competency can provide.

Look for the commonalities which have no division across human lines, and learn from the differences.

If you are working cross-culturally within your company or doing business across borders, you cannot escape this world of global participation. Observe and you will learn. With this awareness, you can see so much more clearly who you are and what part you play. You can become aware of how others perceive you. You can put yourself in another's shoes. Learning is knowledge. Knowledge is power—the power to be free to let go into what *is* instead of wondering why it *isn't*.

Seven Cross-Cultural Inner Quest Steps

- Be adventuresome, be fearless, and see yourself straight on.

- Explore the outer world; be curious and open.

- From the outer world the mind is stimulated, and the heart is opened.

- Be challenged by the unknown; be inquisitive and a perpetual student of life.

- Then find your inner world; go within and explore there.

- Use both worlds, the inner and the outer, to take you on a journey uniquely your own; explore who you are, how you see yourself, and how you might be perceived by someone else of a different culture.

- Become more understanding of others; it will bring you to greater acceptance of yourself too.

SECTION II

A *Guide* for the Journey

LESSON 1

Language Colors What Other People Think

Language is an outward expression of communication through words, but it comes from an inner way of thinking that is different in different cultures. Some thinking is more conceptual, while other kinds are more direct. This can cause problems when doing business internationally.

Language colors *what* people think.
Language colors *how* people think.

Some languages are set up to be more logical or analytical and other languages are set up to be more contextual and conceptual. A logical language has rules and the word means exactly what the word means. But in languages that are more contextual, like Chinese or Japanese, the written language uses pictures or symbols called *ideograms*, which represent concepts and ideas. These are open for interpretation based on the context in which they're used.

Our culture comes through in our language. That's why word-for-word translations are difficult to do and interpretations vary. This is especially so when one of those languages is logical and one is contextual, or one is more poetic and the other is more popular for science.

The linguistic tone or pitch in which something is said also matters in some cases. In tonal languages, you cannot know the exact meaning of a word or phrase without knowing what tone is used to say it. For example, in a Chinese song, it is difficult to grasp meaning without knowing the context ahead of time, because singing changes the normal spoken pitch of words.

When "Yes" Means "No"

To further complicate matters, in certain languages sometimes when people say "yes," they really mean "no" or "maybe." You can tell when "yes" means "no" by looking for nonverbal cues, e.g., if someone says "yes," but shakes their head or looks away.

In a contextual culture, one might say "yes" because saying "no" to a direct question is considered rude. So they're saying "yes," but if you're from that same cultural orientation, you're in that same context, and you're speaking that language, everyone knows it means "no." It's a polite way of saying "no" by saying "yes, but …"

Difficulties arise in communication even when the language spoken is very clear.

If you're speaking a language other than your native tongue, your culture will still influence your way of thinking. You might be thinking contextually, yet speaking in a language that is not contextual, and vice versa.

Individuals have varying cognitive styles which influence how they think, perceive, and remember information.

Some people have a very logical and analytical way of thinking. They line up the processes, the details, and they assume that those details will come to a logical conclusion.

Some people are more results-oriented. They decide what they want and then go backwards to look at which steps need to be implemented to end up with the desired result.

Some people are more generalists and they look at case-by-case scenarios.

Some adapt from time-honored techniques, while others prefer an innovative approach looking beyond what is given.

Different Alphabets

There are many writing systems in the world. Here are a few: You are familiar with the Latin or Roman script (ABCs) used in English and other languages spoken in the Americas, Western Europe, and most of Africa. The Cyrillic script (Кириллица) is used for Russian and languages in Eastern Europe, North Asia, and Central Asia. The Arabic script (العربية) is used in North Africa and Arab countries. The Devanagari script (देवनागरी) is used for Hindi and 120 languages.

These writing systems are based on letters, which represent sounds. As such, these are called syllabary alphabets. Letters and syllables are put together to make words with meanings.

Other languages are based on symbols or characters, which represent concepts. The Japanese and Chinese languages are conceptual and contextual.

I can show you the way. Subway sign with three writing systems in Tokyo, Japan 1978.

The Japanese writing system uses Chinese characters, called *kanji* (漢字)as its foundation for writing. And the Japanese also use two syllabary alphabets. This means the Japanese have three different writing systems.

Other language distinctions color how people think and act. In Japanese, there are 107 ways to say "you," although there are only about four ways most commonly used. "Sex, Status, and Second Person Pronouns" was the topic of my Master's thesis at Jochi Daigaku, Sophia University, in Japan. Why so many ways to say "you"? In German, French and Spanish there are only two, formal and informal.

In Japanese there are also considerations of the sex and status of not only the speaker and the listener, but also who else is within hearing distance. Two people might use one form of "you" when others are in hearing range and another form when in private. As one word for "you" became

30

popularized, it would lose its formality and another word had to be created. For example, the highest form of "you" used to be *anata*, meaning "that place over there," so formal the word could only refer to the space occupied by the revered person and not the person himself. Today however, *anata* is commonly used between friends and couples.

Some Language Questions to Consider

- What language do your international business partners speak?
- Is your language similar or from a different language group?
- Do you notice a great cognitive difference in the way people think when they use English?
- How does this affect your business dealings?

LESSON 2

Techniques for Better Intercultural Communication

How to Speak English to Nonnative English Speakers

Talking with nonnative English speakers requires more awareness in making sure that our words and messages are understood.

The potential for confusion, not being able to find the right words, not being understood, or not understanding the other can lead to embarrassment, misunderstandings, and miscommunications on both sides. This creates stress or impatience at best and can also strain or break business relationships.

English is an international language of business and builds a future for children around the world. "And what is his name?" I ask.

"Make new friends, but keep the old. One is silver and the other gold."
English class at Uzbek school with Mrs. Nargiza and Mrs. Harriet.

Understanding the Nonnative Speaker

English is often the language of multicultural business communication, but it can be difficult to understand the English of nonnative speakers who are not fluent. Their native accent might be strong and your ear may not be used to hearing foreigners speak English.

Verbal communications with others who are not bilingual and whose English is a second language takes patience, relaxation, and openness. When we relax, we are more able to drop expectations and linear thought of how things should be. We can then move into becoming more creative in our way of communicating, hearing beyond the words and into the heart of the meanings.

If we are stuck on needing everything said in proper correct English, we block anything that falls outside of that box and judge it as incorrect.

Focus on what you *do* understand, rather than what you *do not* understand.

Points to Remember for Understanding the Nonnative English Speaker:

- Ask the speaker to talk more slowly.
- Relax and remember to listen and try to understand.
- Repeat what you think the speaker has said.
- Read the speaker's lips.
- Do not interrupt the speaker. Give him or her enough time in which to communicate.
- Listen to everything the speaker has to say before assuming you don't understand.
- Observe body language and other nonverbal signals.
- Beware of a positive response to a negative question.
- Beware of a qualified "yes," in response to the question, "Do you understand?"
- Share responsibility for poor communication.
- If appropriate, invite the speaker to spell difficult words.
- Encourage the nonnative speaker to give a written summary.

English is Not All the Same

If you do have a conversation with someone who speaks English, make sure the English you are speaking is the same.

In Kyrgyzstan, I was once invited to a social dinner. The husband was meeting some former school friends, like a mini-reunion, and the wife wanted me to come along so she had a companion too. I was their houseguest. The translator was their fluent English-speaking daughter who ran an NGO (nongovernmental organization). She had a nondescript accent, leaning towards the U.S. accent rather than a British one.

She translated that I should go to dinner with them. No time had been indicated, so I went out for the day and came back at 4 p.m., with plenty of time to get ready for dinner.

However, when I asked what time we would be leaving, I was told they had already eaten dinner at noon. Dinner for U.S. speakers is in the evening, or a holiday family gathering on a late afternoon, and the midday meal is lunch. She had been using the British meaning of dinner, which is at midday.

And so I missed the luncheon—oh, I mean, dinner. But, fortunately it was not a business meeting. I learned then to not assume anything and to ask clear questions about time.

Jargon

Americans often like to use sports jargon in business. These expressions are so common among fluent English speakers that many forget the expressions *are* jargon—a specialized language. Avoid them.

At a loss for casual conversation? Teach one of these expressions to your foreign counterpart. It could stimulate a cross-cultural dialogue about sports. Here are some examples:

- I'll *touch base* with you next week (contact you)

- Give me a *ballpark figure* (estimated range)
- This is a *home-run* for us (an achievement, a win)
- He has *two strikes against him* already (already made mistakes)
- That seems too *out in left field* (unexpected, unusual)
- This is really *off the wall* (unusual, inappropriate)
- We are *in the big league now* (larger corporate connections)
- Keep your *eye on the ball* (focus on the goal)
- He *dropped the ball* (did not complete the task)
- That was a real *curveball* (surprising, unexpected)
- Did you *cover all the bases*? (be thorough, look at all alternatives)
- *Step up to the plate* (take responsibility)

Here are some other commonly used American English business expressions that are not universal:

- Bottom line
- No way
- ASAP
- We need this yesterday
- R & D
- P & L
- Go over someone's head
- This won't fly
- Cover yourself
- Cement a deal

Take the Positive Approach

See the bigger picture. What is the purpose for communicating at all? We want to connect. We want to develop a relationship that works. Just as you drop the idea that someone needs to look or dress like you do, drop the idea that someone needs to speak your kind of English to be understood. Get creative with your verbal use of words; say it in different ways; look for signs of whether they understand or not. Are they nodding their head? Are they emitting any sounds of acknowledgment (*uhmmm, yes, oh*)?

Use body language and facial expressions to communicate.

When we are not as dependent on spoken words, we naturally develop our nonverbal skills and perceive and understand more than what verbal language may indicate.

You already know how to do this, whether you realize it or not.

For example, when you speak to a young child, your boss, or a new acquaintance, you probably think more carefully about what you say and how you say it. You're probably on your best behavior, more patient, and take your time to listen and speak clearly. Your body posture reflects this.

Of course if you are internally stressed, frustrated, or judgmental, you will diminish your ability to speak consciously, listen, and really hear, and therefore also diminish your chances of understanding and being understood. Your mood and feelings come through in your body language.

Have you noticed that native English speakers from Britain, Australia, New Zealand, use different expressions, colloquialisms, and intonation than those from the U.S.? In India and Jamaica, English carries a more distinct accent and cadence.

Listen carefully to fully understand, or ask questions to clarify.

If we hang on to our concepts of what that difference means, we draw the focus to just the gap, the *difference*.

If we can observe with a witnessing approach—a nonjudgmental awareness without an emotional reaction internally—we are able to look beyond the external differences and see the actual person. We can bridge the gap and start to focus on the *similarities* and the spaces where we can find common ground.

Everyone has a mind and thoughts. We see. We notice. But what we do with the thoughts will impact our ability to communicate, connect, and develop a relationship.

Stop going along with spiraling thoughts. Breathe, relax, and trust. Then you will allow the creativity for communications to come forth.

The ability to do this depends on your personal comfort level, individual personality, your culture, personal past experiences, and exposure to different cultures.

And never underestimate the intelligence of a person just because they are not fluent in *your* language. If you ever wonder, "Why can't they speak English better?" remember English is not their native language. Do you speak their mother tongue? Do you speak any foreign language? Put yourself in their shoes. Imagine yourself in their position.

Points to Remember for Speaking with Nonnative English Speakers

- Speak slowly and distinctly.
- Do not shout. Louder is not clearer.
- Use familiar words.
- Emphasize or repeat keywords.
- Organize your thoughts.
- Do not cover too much information at one time.
- Say exactly what you mean to say.
- Repeat and recap frequently.
- Check for understanding frequently.
- Find alternative ways to say something.
- Allow pauses.
- Be aware of the tone of your voice.
- Let the listener read your lips.
- Use appropriate gestures.
- Take care not to patronize.
- Take care not to laugh inappropriately.
- Watch for nonverbal signs.
- Avoid broken or pidgin English.
- Avoid slang and jargon.
- Avoid jokes.
- Avoid sarcasm.
- Use visual aids.

- Write down important words.

- Do not interrupt to correct.

- Avoid confusing negative questions like "So, you're not going to do that, are you?"

- Be aware of regional English language differences.

- Do not judge someone's intelligence by his or her lack of fluency in English.

LESSON 3

The World is One Family

How a society looks at life depends on whether the culture is based on external or internal control. It is important to understand the differences between these two cultures, and how they view each other, to avoid misunderstandings.

Someone from an *external control culture* is often mistaken for being slow or lacking motivation, while someone from an *internal control culture* can be seen as rash and untrustworthy.

Cultures that are based on the concept of "fate," or external control, feel that there is a predetermined destiny or place for them in society. They therefore feel there's a role for them in their business and on their team, and they are content in that role.

They don't assume that they, individually, are responsible for anything, or that they need to be. If they feel this cultural orientation towards external control or fate, they often feel what is, just is. They base everything on history, on protocol, on formality and they move forward in their business arrangements and operations with that attitude.

There are some cultures that believe there are forces beyond their control—that things are predestined and preset, and this is just the way it's going to be. For businesspeople in most of these cultures, these forces are more powerful than their own individual will or the impact that their company can have on the greater whole of life.

Progress could be slower in discussions with a cultural assumption of external control, because new ideas may not be accepted. There could be a sense of "Oh well, why change it. It's always been that way." They may feel disempowered. Others from cultures with assumptions of internal control may see them as lacking motivation.

On the other hand, cultures that feel they have *internal control* do not feel as dependent on the control of an external force and don't believe that things are set. They feel that they have the power to make change, no matter how small or large. These cultures will see themselves and individuals, and the organizations they work for as in control of future events. Change is possible—and within the lifetime of the person.

Others from external-control cultures may see them as brash, rash, transitory, changeable, and untrustworthy.

Therefore, when you're working with a group of people who come from a culture where they believe that they have internal control and the ability to change the future, it's good to come up with new challenges on future possibilities and prospects in your negotiating. But, with an external control culture, you need to respect past traditions and precedents and know that the outcome of negotiations that happened in the past is important.

Culture-to-Culture Interrelationships

Cultures can be ethnocentric, xenocentric, or polycentric in how they interrelate with other cultures.

Ethnocentrism is the tendency to look at the world primarily from the perspective of one's own culture.

Ethnocentric cultures are very exclusive and do not easily

understand or adapt to other ways of seeing, believing, or operating in the world. They're concerned about their own ethnicity and they prefer to do business with people who are like them. Or, at least they're not used to doing business with people outside of their own ethnicity.

Americans in general are highly ethnocentric. In multicultural terminology, this means we tend to be absorbed in our own cultural ways and expect others to learn our ways in order to communicate and interact.

Ethnocentric cultures judge other cultures by the values and standards of their own culture, especially in regards to language, behavior, customs, and religion.

Ethnocentrism can be overt or subtle, and it is natural in human psychology, but carries a negative connotation in the global sphere.

Xenocentric cultures have a preference for products, styles, or the ideas of another culture or cultures. They do not depend upon their own cultural norms to move forward in business. They prefer to copy or follow other cultural norms.

This is a popular way of thinking in many developing nations where people look up to other cultures as more advanced and disregard the value of their ancestral roots. In a xenocentric society, people want everything new and everything foreign. Modern materialistic goods, like the latest electronics, a TV, fax machine, designer watch, and even foreign friends show status.

In business, marketing and sales, and working with people of other cultures, it is important to understand if they have a strong connection to their history and their culture. Are they are looking to incorporate change but within the dynamic of their own way of being? Or are they ready to jump off and start completely with a new kind of approach to business and economic development?

Obviously, if someone has great pride in their culture and ancient history, a successful approach to doing business would be to respect that culture and work within the dynamics of how they operate. Learn their ways in order to build trust over a period of time. Then you could have a have a beneficial business relationship.

On the other hand, if your culture, your products, your ways and your modern style are what they are aspiring towards, and they're from an xenocentric society, you could probably go into business with very little change to your customs.

Polycentric cultures are very inclusive of other cultures. Their culture overlaps with other cultures, and they move easily between cultures.

In polycentric cultures, people are more routinely exposed to other cultures, so it can be easier to develop working relationships. They may or may not have a deeply-rooted connection to their own native culture, but are open to new ideas and new ways. They will usually take the new ideas and adapt and integrate them into their own culture.

Kyrgyzstan is an example of a society of polycentric people. They are deeply rooted in their 2,000-year-old indigenous culture, one of the oldest in the world, and yet they have been able to expand beyond their culture and embrace other cultures. They were conquered by Genghis Khan, Islam was introduced between the 9th and 12th centuries, and in modern times they were a part of the Soviet Union until their independence in 1991. Currently, they are a small country of 5.7 million who have worked with and hosted both the Russians and the U.S. military within their borders. They speak both Kyrgyz and Russian and study English in school. And yet they retain their native Krygyz culture, shamanistic beliefs, and mixed customs.

Kyrgyz girls wear bows in their hair at the beginning of the school year. This is a Russian custom.

India is another example of a polycentric culture. Indian people are known to embrace all people, cultures and religions. The EME temple in Vadodara, Gujarat, India has the five major religions standing together, to symbolize the oneness and universality of spiritual beliefs.

Indian business practices are also very fluid with other cultures. They are able to straddle the old world of the East and the new world of the West in their business and society. The growth of the middle class in India in the past twenty-five years is a perfect example of their ability to become very worldly, global, fully embracing, and polycentric.

Vasudhaiva Kutumbakam, "The world is one family," is an ancient Sanskrit phrase from the Upanishads, texts containing philosophical concepts of Hinduism. It is engraved in the entrance to the Parliament of India. It indicates that all peoples and all forms of life are to be respected. Any power, large or small, cannot have its way if it disregards others. Narendra Modi, Indian Prime Minister, used this phrase in an interview to a Japanese reporter, adding that, "This is in our DNA, this is in our genetic system." Mahatma Mohandas Gandhi's nonviolent conflict resolution seems to extend from this ancient concept.

Polycentrism is an open attitude towards other cultures and ways of life and opinions. Through polycentrism, we accept intercultural actions and behaviors and start to adapt to them. It's when we interpret them not only through our own cultural experience, but also recognize and appreciate the values of other cultures. We see the whole context that includes more than just our own cultural perception and we learn from this.

Karma

Rotary International clubs in India and around the world serve humanity in need. I visited a Rotary-funded clinic in Vadodara, India.

Rotary 100th Celebration in Udaipur, India. I am here with some members of an all-women's club, joining 2,000 people in the Race for Rotary publicity event.

In India, the sense of *karma* and seva (service) are prevalent in the workplace. If you help someone, someone will help you. The sense of service to humanity is very strong. In India, the team is important. Indians tap into people's natural tendencies instead of just training someone to improve their skills.

For example, if someone is more social, they will be the marketer or salesperson. If someone is not as social, they will be the problem-solvers and researchers behind the scene. The marketer will try something new that the problem solver comes up with. Everyone accepts their role, and time and training are not wasted on trying to make someone different than their natural tendencies. Each person has their way, their *dharma*. They take pride in what they do.

Indians are polycentric. They are inclusive to other peoples, cultures and religions.

Keep in mind whether the culture you are doing business
with is generally ethnocentric, xenocentric or polycentric.

Points to Remember

- Cultures that believe in external control think
  there is a predetermined place for them in society.
  Changes that veer from the norm are not easily
  made.

- Cultures based on internal control believe they
  are in charge of their own destiny.

- Ethnocentric societies judge other cultures by the
  standards of their own culture.

- Xenocentric cultures prefer to copy or follow
  other cultures' norms.

- Polycentric cultures are inclusive of others and
  move easily between cultures.

LESSON 4

Innovative vs. Traditional Cultures

Some cultures are innovative, while others are traditional. This affects how people view and perform with risk—whether they are comfortable with it or avoid it.

Cultures that are more future-oriented and innovative are more at ease with risk. They are comfortable with creation, newness, and change. Among these countries are Denmark, Hong Kong, England, and Singapore.

Traditional cultures are not comfortable with risk, but more at ease with what is already known and what has been done historically. They'll move more slowly with change. Japan, Belgium, China, Russia and France are some of the countries known to be risk-avoidant.

That being said, not all old cultures are traditional cultures.

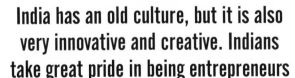

India has an old culture, but it is also very innovative and creative. Indians take great pride in being entrepreneurs and taking risks.

It's important not to stereotype individuals, an entire population, or an entire culture. A culture can be traditional and formal, and forward-thinking and risk-oriented at the same time. Try to keep this in mind before finding ways to approach the culture, do business, negotiate, and build relationships.

Indians are innovative, creative, and hard-working. They will find a niche and be proud of it, telling everyone. One new trend in India is *tiffins*, which is like bento box in Japan, or a complex lunchbox in the U.S. Tiffins are made of stainless steel round containers that stack in layers. Inside each one are multiple sections to keep the food separated.

Two sizes/configurations of tiffins.

Traditionally, a wife packed lunch like this for her husband when he left in the morning, but then the food got cold by the time he ate it.

So, someone started a service to pick up the home-cooked meal at lunch time and deliver it, nice and warm, to the workplace.

In India, roles, skills, and trades are passed down from generation to generation which may seem a traditional orientation. Mentorship provides moral support.

However, in India, there is no set way to do anything. If it does not work out, they keep trying. They do not take it personally, as we might in the U.S., where we are a more individualistic, less collective culture.

My First Time Overseas: Tips for Getting There

My actions reflect my U.S. culture—a highly innovative one. In the context of the following story, you'll see how American cultural orientation interplays with how I think and how I act. In later lessons, you'll also recognize other American cultural norms in this story as well.

When I did not have enough funds to finish college in the U.S., I went to Spain instead. I took control and came up with different ideas to make it work.

TIP: Align with Your Intention

If you want something, and it is right for you, your desire will stimulate your creativity to get it. Even if it is not in the same form, the essence of what you want will come to you.

In my school years, I studied French and Latin. When I went to Boston University, I started learning Spanish. Since Spanish was much more widely spoken in the U.S. and in Latin and South America, I thought it was important to know it. My first Spanish teacher was Cuban and she opened my eyes to the world in many ways. I knew I would become more fluent if I actually immersed myself by living in a Spanish-speaking country, and as a sociology major, I already realized the connection between culture and language.

To keep on target with my education, therefore, I chose to go to the University of Sevilla, Spain.

I had other motivations for going to Spain besides learning the language. I wanted to travel to another country. I had only been to Canada. I grew up in Cleveland, Ohio, which is on Lake Erie. When I was a child, we used to spend time in the summer on our family boat and go to the islands of Lake Erie, especially Kelley's Island, where my grandparents had a cottage.

One time I remember we traveled much further to Pelee Island, on the Canadian side. When my father told me that I was in another country called Canada, I actually got down in the sand on the shore and kissed it. I was so overjoyed to be in a foreign place.

TIP: Look for Other Options

The third and most pressing reason I went to Spain was purely economic. I was putting myself through college and Boston University was expensive.

Even as a full-time student, I worked thirty hours a week. But this was not enough.

The second year, my savings gone, I could not afford all the costs. I bartered with a student for the first semester to live in her space, and in the second semester I was fortunate to get a free room in the dormitory in exchange for being an Area Advisor.

Now it was the third year and I had no further options but to leave school or find a cheaper alternative. I wanted to graduate from Boston University, so I found I could go overseas for a year to the Universidad de Sevilla, and then transfer the credits back. It would be half the cost and I would have a life adventure and come back with Spanish-speaking fluency.

I had taken extra credits in Spain, so to complete the fourth year, I enrolled in summer term upon my return to Boston, a cheaper alternative, and was able to graduate one semester early, eliminating that tuition altogether.

Perhaps this was the beginning of my entrepreneurial and negotiating skill set.

TIP: Reach Out for Help

I arrived in Spain on a Sunday when everything was closed. I only had the address of the university and the phone number of the Director of the orientation language program I was to take before university classes began. I did not know how to use the pay phone, and besides, I had no coins. And my Spanish was very limited. No internet and no mobile phones in the 1972. Fortunately, I saw some Spanish students, and one of them spoke rudimentary English. Communication happened, a phone call was made, and I was walked to the home of the Director within the hour.

Most people are responsive to those in need.

TIP: Reason and Resolve

If you have an idea that is logical and fills all the requirements, put it forth and make it happen. Look at what the final result needs to be and show how your idea will get that result.

When I was settled in with my Spanish family, I received room and board in exchange for conversing with the children in English for two hours a day. The family had just relocated from England and the parents did not want the children to lose their English speaking ability. However, two hours a day soon became all the time I was not at school, so I knew after a few days that this would not work out for me. How would I learn Spanish well without opportunities to practice it?

The Program Director did not have any other options for me. And there was a rule that we had to live with a Spanish family. I was in a quandary.

Then, one day, I met Violeta at school. She was from a small village and new to Sevilla. There was a two-bedroom apartment available in which one room had three Spanish students already committed to it, and the smaller bedroom was available for two. So, we roomed together. Rules were in place. No men allowed, except in the living room only to pick us up to go out, not to hang out there.

I went to the Director and said, "Look. I have a great opportunity to share an apartment with four female students who do not know any English. I will be living there unless you can come up with a Spanish family to live with where I can speak Spanish."

And I moved in.

TIP: Keep Trying

Go through the transition and know you will come out to the sunshine at the end of the tunnel.

For the first month, I struggled with learning Spanish. One day between my tearful sobs, I told a student from Colombia, "I just want to express my feelings and get to know people in depth." He replied "You will. Just keep trying." And I did.

TIP: Offer Creative Solutions to Get What You Need

Business negotiation can be creative. It then becomes relational and not just transactional.

By the end of the semester, I could speak Spanish really well, but my grammar and writing were more elementary. When speaking, there are nonverbal hints in the look on someone's face that can help verify whether or not you are understood. And there is an opportunity to ask questions and rephrase for clarity. Therefore, I made a deal with my professors. If I could take all the exams orally in the first semester, I would take all the exams, first and second semester, in writing at the end of the year.

I met the exam requirements, but in a different way. Success was mine. I got straight As.

TIP: Find Unique Situations

What makes you and your experiences different than someone else in your business? Find some unique quality that sets you apart from the norm.

We were the first group of North Americans to be at the University of Sevilla, Spain. This unique situation allowed for a lot of interaction with curious Spanish students who became new friends, especially because some of our culture and customs were excitingly different.

LESSON 5:

Long-Term vs. Short-Term Cultures

Some cultures think long-term, while others think short-term. This affects how they develop business relationships and view obligation, interdependence, and lifelong connections.

I find one of the foundational principles of cross-cultural business dynamics to be whether someone thinks long- or short-term.

Cross-cultural understanding between long-term and short-term cultures is really about understanding that what we (in a short-term culture) may see as progress is different than what others (in a long-term culture) see as progress.

We have to get beyond judgments based on our values and look through the eyes of the other culture; that takes cross-cultural expertise.

Do your homework, and if you don't know, ask someone who does know. I am here to guide you on your journey.

It is very typical of the American culture to think short-term. We may have five, ten or twenty-year plans, but our way of doing business is short-term-oriented compared to many other cultures. We want to see results right now, right away. We want our meetings to be short and efficient. We're looking at results on paper and for the movement of the economics of the business, the sale of the product or a contract.

Progress in a long-term orientated culture will be based on the relational connections that are made at the right level in the hierarchy. We do not necessarily put the same value upon developing the relationship that other cultures might.

There are many reasons for this. One is that our lives are very mobile. We're not expected to be in the same job for our whole lives.

The degree of formality and informality may overlap short-or long-term thinking.

For example, going into a business arrangement with a Northern European would typically involve a very direct, informal approach. Everyone there knows they want to do business together and gets down to it immediately. You may or may not even go to lunch.

It's efficient. It's quick. And it has a conclusion right away. Northern European culture is not based on developing a relationship. It is based on which business deal looks the best at the time, and whether or not it matches the needs of the two partners. It's usually a win-win situation based on price, product, and time.

However, in many cultures, you need a relationship with someone before doing business with them. Once you enter a relationship, there's an obligation that goes with it. When you enter a relationship, it's assumed that relationship is going to be long-lasting.

Therefore, people do not randomly start a business relationship unless they really know a person. Really knowing a person means long meals, lots of entertaining, months, even years of a little bit of business and a lot of waiting. It takes a long time to develop relationships, but once they are made, they are for life.

For a person who comes from a short-term orientation (like the Americans) to do business with a culture that's long-term-oriented takes observation, patience, patience, and patience. But if you're long-term oriented and you can see that this is moving towards something, you can develop that patience as you develop trust.

So if you think you're not getting anywhere in long-term-oriented business development or negotiations, trust that you are. Every meeting, every meal, every back and forth is taking you there. I hear from my clients over and over, "Why do we have to have another meeting?" "What are they doing in those meetings anyway?" "They seem like they're falling asleep." But the fact that there even is a meeting is progress in itself.

Need for Constant Contact

Although social media are globally used and on the rise, the need to use social media daily is very Westernized. The idea that we need to be in contact on a daily basis is short-term thinking. Just because we lose connection with someone today doesn't mean we have lost the connection forever.

We may feel that we've lost touch with a customer or client or someone if we haven't heard from them in a year or two. We may feel that unless we get a quick answer to our proposal or an email, this indicates a lack of interest.

However, if we look from a different perspective, this doesn't necessarily mean what we might think it does. To answer an email right away might not be practical in the culture we're dealing with, because they may need to have a consensus from their group before they're even allowed to give an answer.

So when dealing with other cultures, the idea of getting an immediate response causes impatience on one side and wonderment on the other about why you would need an answer right away.

Connecting and Reconnecting

Americans network, make introductions to others, and go to lunch to get to know each other's businesses in order to help and create mutual exchanges or leads for the future. We keep connecting and reconnecting.

In long-term cultures, there's not this need to constantly reconnect. You can call in a favor five, ten, twenty years later from someone. Spain is one of those cultures.

Once you're in, you're in. But to get in, it takes a while. It's like family. You have to become part of the family, and once you're in, you're in for life.

When I moved from Sevilla, Spain, I was told "You are family...forever." I have kept in touch with my Spanish family for forty years. Members of my American family have been to Spain and members of my Spanish family have spent summers in the U.S.

On my last visit, my Spanish sister made the pineapple upside-down cake from the recipe I had given her forty years ago. And I found Violeta my old roommate. Such a delight.

Japan is like that. China is like that. In these cultures, it is not difficult to reconnect even after many years.

Value of Interdependence

Japanese relationships are long-term. Their interdependence develops a sense of not only obligation, but also dependence with a deeper connection.

Americans are individualistic and take pride in our independence and being able to succeed on our own accord. For the Japanese, if you do not make dependent relationships, you do not relate.

After evening meetings, if not sent home by taxi, I was always taken not only to the train station, but also accompanied a few stops further, if not all the way. And not for my safety, as Tokyo is one of the safest cities in the world. Then why? I used to insist I lived there, knew my way and could surely get home without their help.

Until a close friend replied, "You need to be more *amae*." *Amae* also means "sweet" like in food. To be sweet, is to be dependent. My independent self asked, "Why?" He replied, "Because then you will give us the opportunity to help you." It was not about my capabilities or needs, but rather about the interconnectedness, creating that interdependence and giving someone else the chance to help, be it needed or not.

It was to allow someone else into my world by just being there. It was the route to the long-term relationship of giving and receiving over and over again.

Obligation—Just the Right Degree

There's a degree of obligation when developing a relationship with someone, and you want the right balance to make it comfortable for all.

I was introduced to Yoko Ono Lennon in the U.S. by the Director of the largest yoga and wellness facility where I worked. I was going to Japan for a few months to make arrangements for the Director's three-week seminar tour there. Yoko's brother lived in Japan, so she gave me his contact information. He helped by introducing me to a graphic artist and PR man who put together my promotional materials. And he treated me as the honored guest to a couple dinners. Obligation met.

Nothing more.

The degree of both my relationship and the Director's with Yoko Ono was minimal, and not long-term. We had only met her once. Therefore, the degree of the favor from her brother was limited. Everyone and everything in its place.

Favors Are Not Forgotten in Long-Term Relationships

In Tokyo, I was on special assignment for several months being trained in the nonferrous metal division of Nissho Iwai Corporation (now Sojitz Corporation).

Why was I allowed to be the first and only non-Japanese outsider to be allowed to see the inner workings of Nissho Iwai?

It went way back to an old favor and a *giri* (obligation) that was only now being paid back or called in. Twenty years previously, a young rising Japanese manager who spoke English well, was sent by Nissho Iwai to be trained in the London office of the German Metallgesellschaft (MG) conglomerate. Twenty years later, as a young head of MG's Japan Desk in New York City, I was sent to Nissho Iwai Tokyo to be trained.

That obligation lasted twenty years and not only went beyond the decision-makers at the time to a new generation of executives, but also beyond countries.

So here I was in Tokyo again, where I had lived and worked previously for five years.

My situation was unique. Most foreign businesspeople only knew some basic Japanese words, enough to tell the taxi which way to go. I spoke the language, and had my master's degree from a top Japanese university. Other foreigners lived in expatriate segregated communities, whereas I had lived in total immersion in a Japanese neighborhood.

I did not fit into the pigeonhole of a typical short-term visit, non-Japanese-speaking Westerner. Therefore, I was treated on my own merit. And I had developed connections the Japanese way.

Following Their Lead

My mentor was the gentleman who had gone to London to train in MG twenty years before. To have a mentor is traditionally Japanese and a big boon.

I was introduced to the Japanese *kacho* (managers) who spoke English and started observing their daily functions and work life. They all knew my background through my resume.

They spoke to me in English, even though I was in Japan, even though everyone else was Japanese, and even though they knew I was fluent in Japanese…for three whole weeks. Then all of a sudden, one day, everyone just switched over to Japanese, and nothing was ever mentioned.

This was a testing period. By just following their lead, I spoke English when spoken to in English, and switched to Japanese only when they did first. This showed respect and an ability to be humble on my part.

I was treated with respect and professionalism in Nissho Iwai. Now I was part of the daily life of the company for the duration of my stay. I was exceptionally fortunate to not only learn their processes, but also to have a mentor to answer my questions, and personal Japanese friends and connections from my previous residency who could tell me the inside scoop of Japanese business relations.

One Act of Kindness Leads to a Lifelong Connection

We are a host family for the Council of International Programs (CIP USA). In 2006, one simple act— inviting two female artisans from Kyrgyzstan into our home for a few weeks—led to my soul-searching journey to their country for three months two years later.

I was at a point in my life where I wanted to stop reminiscing about my travels across the Marco Polo Silk Route thirty-three years previously and create new adventures in this moment of time. My goal was to go to a place where I had never been, far away, in a developing nation with a very distinct culture from my own that had a different language and writing script. Wow. Did ever I hit the jackpot—"Krygyzstan, here I come!"

For one year, I added twenty hours a week to my full-time work in order to study Russian at a local college before going overseas.

CIP made an email introduction to Gulasel, head of the national Kyrgyz Land Council of International Fellowship, part of CIP. She met me at the airport, arranged my housing outside Bishkek at her friend Burma's apartment, and helped me during my three months there.

Plans Change—New Opportunities Appear

All my plans fell through.

After arriving, the woodworking institute where I was to teach and coach small business owners closed. Like many, the owner moved his family back to Russia.

So I found other opportunities to volunteer my time and expertise while traveling the entire country. I met Jamilya, who arranged seminars for social workers interested in learning stress management techniques. I met the elite through the Rotary Club, urban Bishkek residents and office workers, and rural artisans who had visited Ohio as I traveled village to village. Like passing the buckets of water for a fire down the line of people, I was put in a long-distance taxi or on a bus by friends at one end and greeted by others at the other end, everything seamlessly coordinated between them by mobile phones.

I traveled to Isfana, the farthest village in southeastern Kyrgyzstan. It was in a part of the country where even the Peace Corps were not allowed to go because of past border skirmishes with Uzbekistan. I was hosted by a local family whose two daughters, Rakhat and Gulkaiyr, guided me.

Rakhat, Gulkaiyr and friends enjoyed daily yoga class with me after school.

Invited as a guest presenter at their school, the news got around and I found myself teaching both English and yoga daily at several Kyrgyz and Uzbek schools. I held a day-long coaching session for English teachers, sharing materials and ideas, and encouraged them to form the Association of English Teachers in Isfana. I started a small English learning library there.

I met teachers who were fluent in English, yet had never spoken to a native speaker, Mr. Doran and Mrs. Mohira.

They called me Mrs. Harriet. And they told me my name sounded like Hariet in Kyrgyz, which means "Gift of God" or "Thanks to God." How humbling.

An unexpected invitation to teach a boys' yoga class in Batken Oblast, Kyrgyzstan.

Uzbek teachers in Isfana, Krygyzstan welcome me.

English class students with teachers Mrs. Mohira and me, Mrs. Harriet.

And then three years later, Rakhat came to live with us for a year in Ohio, attending our local Columbia Station High School. This further established the long-term relationship, which will always exist.

Rakhat is now in medical school in Kyrgyzstan. She has two sets of parents, and we have a daughter. We email, write, and Skype. One day we will travel to Kyrgyzstan and see her and her family again.

I continue to send English books and audio books to the library project, called Venture from The Heart. This year, Mrs. Mohira will visit us in Ohio. I now have a lifelong connection to friends in a country far away, yet so close to my heart.

Once met, never forgotten.

Go Off the Beaten Track

These stories do not have to be yours. You do not have to go to a developing nation, out in the wilderness, or even outside of your own country. Just go a bit further off the path already trodden and find a moment of newness, an interaction that helps you become more aware, more open.

Points to Remember for Lasting Business Relationships

- In long-term cultures, you don't have to be in constant contact.

- Interdependence develops a sense of obligation and deeper connection.

- Eat, drink and be merry.

- Get to know your business counterparts.

- Ask them about their lives, their culture.

- Learn to say *hello*, *goodbye* and *thank you* in their language.

- Be in the moment. Enjoy the present.

- How you are now directs the energy for the future.

- Be timeless, not time-bound.

- Smile. Be grateful.

LESSON 6

Formal vs. Informal Cultures

Some cultures are informal and some are formal. Some people take time with business rituals and others favor business efficiency. There are more reserved cultures and more emotional cultures.

The concept of "Belly Art in Business" is about connecting to your gut (for more on this see Lesson 17).

In some cultures, it's more important to be efficient than to be formal or ritualistic. Let's just get on with business. Here's my card. There's your card. Why take five minutes staring at it? There's no need for introductions or formalities. We're here to do business. Let's just sit down and start.

In other cultures, ritual, ceremony, and formality are important.

There is a whole process of even getting your foot in the door. After a proper introduction there's the formality of drinking tea, the bowing or handshakes, exchanging business cards, the need to go out to entertain and have a meal together and not talk business at all, just as a ritual— to begin. To some cultures that can seem like a waste of time.

Long-Term Rewards

In Japan while at Nissho Iwai, I had to go out after work with each team to develop a bonding relationship. This is called *nemawashi* which means "root binding." If you're thinking long-term and you want to bond with the team, it takes time. It takes time to establish a long-lasting relationship.

My suggestion is to breathe deeply, relax and be patient. Because the rewards you will get from developing the relationship in a slow, ritualistic process not only shows respect for their culture, but also acts as a way to get your foot in the door, and you will find long-term rewards in the end.

That being said, you will sometimes find that people from formal societies really like coming over to your culture on your territory, on your turf, and doing business, because they can let their hair down a little bit, loosen up their tie, be a little bit less formal, and feel as if they can get out of the strain of having to be suppressed into a formal structure. So it goes both ways.

They'll appreciate your informality in the right environment and situation which is on your cultural turf. And, you can appreciate their formality when you are in their country and their offices. No one expects you to be different than who you are, but being patient and respectful is something that's easily acquired for the end goal of developing a long-term business relationship.

Emotions in Business

Some cultures are more reserved in expressing their emotions. It is considered bad form, rude, and immature to display emotion in front of others.

That being said, in other cultures it's quite acceptable to be confrontational, to argue, to go back and forth, to have a little bit of animation in a business meeting. It's the way they communicate. In Latin, Indian, and Arab cultures conversations can get quite animated.

However, in East Asian cultures, reserve and nonemotional display are paramount.

Therefore, people will socialize and go drinking after work to let go, de-stress, and talk more freely. But they can never do that in the formal business setting.

In India, showing emotions is common, more so than in the U.S. and definitely more so than in Japan. However, I have found the Indians express their feelings and then quickly move on. They do not seem to hold grudges. What was, was. What is, is. There seems to be an acceptance of individual human nature that does not impede relationships.

In some cultures, you're not allowed to express your individual opinion. You can only speak for what the voice of the consensus is.

Other cultures want people to express themselves individually. The business meeting is exactly for that purpose so each person in the group is able to speak their piece, to get all the ideas out.

In some cultures, there are certain protocols regarding who speaks first and who won't speak at all. It can be very disarming to a person from a more formal culture to go into a meeting with a group of people from the Netherlands, for example, where it's so egalitarian that everyone speaks exactly what is on their mind and there is no leader.

It's a very democratic kind of process. So understanding these differences is also important.

The Two Faces of the Japanese

In Japan, *tatemai* and *honne* are the external "public" face and the internal "private" face.

For me, the Japanese have the best service in the world. From the elevator ladies in the department stores with their white gloves, to the hostesses in kimono waiting with a hot towel as you exit the restroom, the polite face is always on, and there is a ritual in every small action. The private face takes the mask off only at home or under the influence of alcohol.

Being observant, watching and listening, and getting to know the Japanese is important to be able to distinguish between what is shown and what is really happening in business.

The Japanese are private with their personal emotions. To become emotional in business meetings is considered immature and bad form. It is very stressful to hold the emotions in, but the Japanese have a lifetime of practice.

Questions and comments in English need to be more vague and roundabout when doing business in Japan, like the Japanese language itself. No confrontation or putting someone in an awkward position. Hinting, suggesting, humbling oneself, asking for advice and help are acceptable ways to find out information. However, in Japanese business, schedules, final agreements, terms, and pricing are very exact.

When I worked for Encyclopaedia Britannica, Inc. in Japan, I was in charge of hiring and training English teachers for home study programs and I also wrote the book *How to Teach English to the Japanese*. One thing I learned was that business is business. Although I met the CEO and his hiring managers in a social setting, the purpose for the meeting was for me to be introduced to them for the job offer. Our personal relationship was never discussed after I was hired. I was hired for my abilities, education, and job qualifications. We were then on a last name basis. Work life and private life are separate in Japan.

On business trips, even though there was always a meal and entertainment and we got to know each other better, propriety and professionalism within social business engagements were always observed. And there was always a secretary or another woman from the team who accompanied the male managers so that I was not the only female. We laughed, we drank, we bonded, but we were still on business. It felt to me like a work family. Companies often have annual company retreats for a weekend overnight at a hot springs resort with an evening show. The company's employees de-stress and relax. Spouses of either sex do not attend. Even in this setting, it is still business bonding.

I enjoyed the food and relaxation at this company retreat in Japan in 1992.

Japanese do not invite other businesspeople to their homes unless they are close friends. Japanese feel their homes are too small to entertain Westerners.

Business after-hours entertainment is held in public places or private clubs or host/hostess bars (for more on these kinds of bars, see Lesson 16).

Points to Remember: Formal and Informal Interactions

- If you are coming from an informal culture, be patient and respectful when dealing with formal societies.

- Some cultures are intentionally verbally vague, so make sure you listen and observe to pick up what is really being said.

- Do not confront or put someone in an awkward situation.

- Observe others.

- When in doubt, formal is better.

- Formal cultures have more rituals in business

LESSON 7

Relational vs. Transactional Cultures

In some cultures, developing a relationship with the people you are doing business with is most important. Selling the product comes second. But in other cultures, the transaction is the focus, the main goal. Whether you have developed a relationship with those you are doing business with (or not) is irrelevant. Doing business with ease overseas means understanding the differences between transaction- and relationship-focused cultures.

In relationship-oriented cultures, giving business to a friend is more important than getting the best price for your product.

Transaction-oriented cultures want to sell a product at a certain price, or get the best deal within a certain timeframe. It doesn't matter who's executing it. It doesn't matter if you like the person you are buying from. It doesn't matter if you've ever been to a business lunch with them.

These two opposite ways of thinking and doing business can cause misunderstandings. Sometimes relationship-oriented cultures are perceived as stalling, because they're beating around the bush. They are testing the waters. And this can be misinterpreted as being dishonest or untrustworthy.

On the other hand, from the perspective of a relationship-based culture, a transaction-based culture can be seen as pushy, aggressive, not caring about the person or the relationship, and just wanting to complete the deal and then leave.

Relationship-oriented cultures may not want to do business with someone who acts that way because, where's the future? They have the time and the patience to look at a bigger picture.

That being said, people from transaction-oriented cultures are under pressure to constantly produce bottom-line results for the company, the shareholders, and the quarterly reports on a very short-term basis. It's difficult to come from a transaction-oriented culture with the economics and the business we have in the U.S. and say, "Oh, but I'm going to have a twenty-year relationship with this client company. Give me a year to develop it." It's not easily accepted, and fewer people understand the cultural dynamics.

Belarus is a very relational culture. The U.S. is very transactional.

Building Cross-Cultural Business Relationships That Last

I presented at the Council for World Affairs in Cleveland, Ohio for a group of professionals from Belarus. I met Inna. We kept in touch.

A year later, she met her goal and launched the first Coach Federation of Belarus. I was invited to speak at their first conference weekend in Minsk, the capital. There was no funding to pay me or cover my expenses.

Instead, I made a short video in Russian and English. I included encouragement about how wonderful the coaching profession is and that I hoped to see them the following year. They showed it as a welcome piece.

I took my personal time to help them out. I came up with a creative solution.

Although I could not go to Belarus in person, I did the next best thing—a short video— and it was a good marketing tickler for the next year. I was building a foundation, a connection, and when the time was right I knew we'd see each other again in person.

Because of our developing relationship over those past two years, Inna went the extra mile to get funding for me to go to Belarus.

She went to the United States Embassy in Minsk and I was awarded a U.S. AID speaker grant from the State Department. The embassy made all the arrangements, and they also made my very full schedule.

Coach University: Training session in Minsk, Belarus.

Coach University: Inna and me.

Now I was not only going to be going to the new Coach University, but I also became involved in larger projects, organizations, and associations as a keynote speaker, giving several different presentations a day, including at the Bel-Biz week-long entrepreneurship forum. I was the only woman on a panel discussion in front of hundreds of people from Estonia and Ukraine, to Russia and Belarus. I was also the only noneconomist/banker.

I was on stage with a headset with instantaneous translation for me to understand everything that was said in Russian, and for the participants to understand my comments. My motivational speech was about the nature of entrepreneurship and small business ownership, the rewards and challenges, the passion and the integrity.

The Americans from the Embassy were there, I was told the KGB was there, my new acquaintances were there, and I was totally present.

Afterwards, someone came up to me and said it was really inspiring to see a woman onstage. Although the audience was full of women, men dominated the financial realms as bankers, economists, and government officials.

Another person told me they were inspired because I spoke from the heart, and they saw the heart and soul do not have to be ignored in order to be a successful businessperson.

Onstage at the Bel-Biz Entrepreneurship Forum in Minsk, Belarus.

I was so exhilarated the whole time even with full days of speaking engagements and training sessions. I was only away one week and I hardly remembered how I got there. When I came home, I could not believe that it really happened.

Five years later, I am still in touch with several people I met in Belarus, continuing to be relational and not transactional.

Points to Remember: Working in a Transactional Culture

- Get right down to business.
- Speak directly without small talk.
- Do not expect to be entertained.
- Talk in concrete facts and figures.
- Correspond only when necessary.

Points to Remember: Working in a Relational Culture

- Do not bring up business until they do.
- Expect to eat a meal together.
- Observe nonverbals and inferred language.
- Take your time to get to know your counterparts.
- Keep in touch.

LESSON 8

Collective vs. Individualistic Cultures

Cultures can be categorized as collective or individualistic. Individualistic cultures value an individual's hard work, while collective cultures believe in teamwork. This affects how people communicate and interrelate, business decisions, and project management.

In an individualistic culture, people are hired according to their individual abilities and achievements. There is great pride in working independently, making your own way through life, pulling yourself up by your bootstraps, and taking responsibility for both your mistakes and your accomplishments.

Individual initiative is rewarded. Standing out and rising above the crowd is a goal and considered an achievement. Being singled out for what you've done and being rewarded and recognized for it is acceptable. Taking responsibility for mistakes individually made is also part of it. Being independent is risky because there may not be a group norm to follow. There's no rule book. Anything goes. And because of its risk, the individualistic culture is more comfortable with change.

Highly individualistic cultures include the U.S., Canada, Australia, England, France, Italy, Netherlands, Denmark, Sweden, and Israel. Some collective cultures include Japan, China, Central Asia, and most of South and Central America. Of middle orientation are Russia, India, Philippines, Brazil, Chile, and Arab countries.

The individualistic society values, even expects, the individual to be independent. This is accentuated in the upbringing of children when they are taught how to do things for themselves, make their own choices, earn their own money, and not to depend too heavily on others.

My father taught me about money and independence at five years old. I received a nickel for my weekly allowance. And I learned how to spell r-e-s-p-o-n-s-i-b-i-l-i-t-y. All within the context of candy and small toys, I was taught about saving and delaying gratification, as well as borrowing to satisfy immediate desire.

As a comparison, in a collectivist culture, children are indulged, needs are taken care of, and interdependence is the societal norm in adulthood. In Thailand, when someone is in a wheelchair, everyone helps to lift the person, chair and all, up over inaccessible areas.

In an individualistic society, like the U.S., we are not sure if someone really wants help and are concerned that if we do offer help, they might be offended at our assuming their loss of independence.

Interdependence

In a collective society, depending on other people is comfortable and expected. It's a dependence on the group that is your comfort for your life. You have a group that you're dependent on and they are dependent on you. It's a collectivist approach in which people give each other opportunities to help and serve one another. If you become too independent, you take away the opportunity for another person to help you and serve you.

This interdependence is also seen in business. The team is collective. People are checking with each other all the time, because no one wants to stand out individually. Everyone owns a piece of the whole. People play different roles, but each person is included in the information. No decision is made until the collective has made a decision, as a unit, and then that decision is communicated to the business partner or outside company.

That's why getting an answer can take a long time. No single person is your lead from whom you can get the information. He or she has to wait to get the information from someone else. Even the top bosses may articulate the decision, but they don't make the decisions themselves. Before passing information on, they collect it bottom-up and then top-down until everyone shares the information as a unit.

An individual won't stand out and give information prematurely. It's not their role. It's not anyone's role. They're just working as a collective entity. Pride is to be part of the collective unit.

It's not the same pride as in an individualistic culture. The team might respond, "Wow. That person has a great idea. It's innovative. It's different. It's new. Good for coming up with that, Joe!"

However, in a collective society, the person will present the idea in way that implies non-ownership. Then everybody has a piece of it and reworks it. So in the end, it doesn't even look like it came from one person.

It is very indirect, very vague, very behind the scenes. Always caring about saving face for each person, making sure that everything is like one unit. It's comfortable.

Mixing Professional and Personal Life

In the U.S., we do not formally network professionally outside of the workplace unless we are specifically attending a networking event, club or association meeting. This is not the same for each individual, however, and varies in different parts of the country. Usually, Americans tend to leave the workplace, go home and have a private life. We prefer to separate the personal and professional, even in our workplace conversations, until we develop a closer friendship.

Some cultures separate work and private life even more than Americans, while others integrate personal and professional life together.

India is a blend between individualism and collectivism. However, businesses are mixed with family and community life. Indians invest all their resources in a business and then reach out to the whole community to let them know what they do and what they offer. It is their livelihood, from the street peddlers all the way up to corporate CEOs. Indians take pride in their jobs.

Japan is highly collective. Even the company has a paternalistic overtone. When a salaryman is not performing well on the job, it is possible someone could call his wife and very indirectly hint that the home-life needs to be peaceful, just in case it is family or marital troubles that are distracting him.

Points to Remember: Individualistic Cultures

The individual has daily decision-making power.

The individual takes pride in his or her own part.

Independence is seen as a strength.

Private and professional life are separate.

Points to Remember: Collective Cultures

Decisions take time.

The team, department, or company are the identity.

Standing out from the group is undesirable.

Community life is strong.

LESSON 9

Humility vs. Self-Promoting Cultures

What do you feel about humility in business? In the U.S. business context, we are comfortable with self-promotion, while in other cultures it is considered abrasive.

In dealing with some cultures, we have to sell ourselves and promote ourselves.

We have to say what we've done, what our accomplishments are, and why we're the right person to do business with. (Self-promoting cultures tend to be independent cultures; if we are more independent, who is there to promote us? We have to do it ourselves.)

The use of the words "I" and "my" is very common. We talk about ourselves, about that in which we take pride and what we have done.

Business networking clubs are a great example of this. At their events, you introduce yourself, explain very briefly what you do and what you have to offer, and you have to say it with pride, so that the other person will understand that you have what it takes. Then they get a turn to say it back.

Everyone's on the same page, because everyone's doing it.

In dealing with other cultures, for example in Asia, self-promotion is not considered a good quality. Humility is key. This can be tied into the idea of a collective group or an individualistic group. If we're part of a collective team, no one needs to self-promote because the team is what counts.

Speaking about yourself and about your accomplishments is considered rude and not proper in such a culture. It's simply not done. Someone else has to talk about you. A third person needs to promote you, introduce you, and tell others about your achievements.

This sense of humbleness comes forth in many different ways.

When to Decline or Accept an Offer

For example, let's imagine you are offered a cup of tea or coffee and you really don't want it. You respond, "No, no thank you. Let's just get on with business." For one culture, this exchange is viewed as a straightforward question and reply, but in another culture it could be considered rude to not allow the connection to happen with this simple ritual.

A Kyrgyz artisan carpetmaker named Sharapat hosted me in her home for three weeks. When she offered tea several times per day, it seemed like the most important thing to do. It was almost a command, saying, "Stop working, learning, writing down things, and come sit, now."

Humility comes in many different forms. For example, one might offer a seat or gift to another. The humble person might respond by still standing, waiting for a second invitation to sit, or feigning refusal of the gift—"No, no, no. I am not worthy of it"—or having a verbal back and forth with "no-thank-yous" and "pleases" until finally accepting. It's up to the giver to keep offering. It's a kind of game, rather a ritual of pro-offering and refusal, until after two or three tries it is accepted graciously.

Someone could spend hours and hours making a presentation or preparing a meal. The guests repeatedly compliment how all is wonderful, and the host or hostess deflect compliments by saying, "It was nothing. No trouble at all." This self-deprecation that puts oneself down is to be seen in a holistic view.

By putting yourself down, you are raising the other person up.

If both people are from the same culture, they understand exactly what is happening. But when viewed from the outside by a person from a different culture, it can be confusing.

It's a two-sided coin. In the Western cultures, if you decline an offer, it's with an understanding that it will not be offered to you a second time.

However, if somebody is from a different culture, they'll think you're unfriendly or rude by not offering again. Understanding that is important.

At a private party during a convention, the French host offered my colleague some champagne as he arrived, which he politely declined. The Frenchman was taken aback and gave him a cold shoulder. His expression seemed to say, "What, you don't want our hospitality?" My colleague told me if the host had offered again in five minutes he would have accepted, since he had just arrived and wanted to get settled first. How do you think this could have been handled?

Saving Face

Along with the idea of humility comes the idea of saving face. Everyone knows what saving face is, but do you really understand the implications of it? Of course, embarrassing someone in front of others is unacceptable. But where does it begin and where does it stop?

In some cultures, to criticize a person in front of their team is okay, because the boss is often hardest on the most promising and productive of the team members. It's a motivational tactic.

In some cultures, criticism is taken the same way as praise. And ideas, whether good or not, are just opinions. No one cares. Everybody just says what they mean, and that's no problem.

But in another culture, such as Japan, the need for humility and saving face is so strong that even the language itself is indirect and vague. People who are within the same culture understand what is being said, but since it's never said directly, it saves face. And people will sometimes go outside the group to a third-party to convey information that is potentially embarrassing, so that it never causes a confrontation.

A typical example of this is the old go-between in marriage, which now is more often replaced with computer-generated dating services. The matchmaker has a very important role. It's not just about getting the introduction. It's about being the person the couple or families go to when problems arise, so the go-between can gracefully and indirectly pass the message along. That way, they save face by avoiding direct confrontation. Harmony in the family ensues.

Important to note is that a person speaking a vague or indirect language will come across as skirting the truth, being sneaky, or untruthful to a person who is accustomed to speaking more directly unless the differences in these communication styles are understood.

Communication that singles people out, or shows someone rising above the group, is also a way to lose face.

When I was in Japanese graduate school and a quarter-page article with my photograph was published in the daily *Asahi Shimbun* newspaper, the third-largest in the world. It featured me as the first non-Japanese graduate from Jochi Daigaku, Sophia University's Master's degree program. I was also interviewed on the Japanese "Good Morning" show *Ohayo Gozaimasu*. I remember I was proud of my achievement, but on the one hand I was embarrassed.

In my American culture, this would have been a point of pride and my friends would rally around me saying "That's great, Harriet. Look you got your picture in the paper. Good job. Good job."

Some of my Japanese colleagues understood and were quite congratulatory.

However, I heard a few were displeased because I'd been singled out from the group of eighteen. It was a more complex situation because the reality was, I was different and I was singled out for this reason. The other reality is that we all went to the school together. Everyone could have been the team in the newspaper, but then it wouldn't have been a unique story.

HARRIET RUSSELL EARNS MASTER'S DEGREE FROM SOPHIA UNIVERSITY
ASAHI DAILY NEWSPAPER   TOKYO, JAPAN   APRIL 21, 1980

Asahi Shimbun newspaper article. Tokyo, Japan 1980.

Saving Face All Around

At one time I worked in a small Japanese import-export company, a part of the larger Seibu Group. My job was to ensure that communications in English with other countries were properly done. My associate, Chizuko, a young, fluent English-speaking Japanese woman, and I, a fluent Japanese-speaking American, worked together on the Indian carpet imports and correspondences. Our boss, a woman and second-in-command, also knew English, but she had learned it post-war from American movies.

Her fluency was limited in comparison to my associate, who had traveled abroad and lived in the U.S. for six months. But there was the issue of saving face. The boss is to be respected and is always right.

So, we would draft a letter in fluent English. Then I would stand before the boss's desk and show it to her. She would say "This phrasing was not correct English." I would humbly reply, "Oh. I am from Ohio. Perhaps there are other ways to say it. Excuse me." Then my colleague and I would seemingly correct the letter, really making it incorrect, and show her again. What really happened was this: We would send the original letter that my colleague and I had drafted to the Indian carpet companies, so our company would not lose face with inferior correspondence. We would keep a copy of the boss's corrected version in the files, to save her face. All was well all around. Face was saved for everyone.

By the way, that was not my idea. That was my colleague's idea, so it must have been a Japanese way.

Learning a Lesson while Saving Face

Saving face in Japan and helping others save face is as important as following rules and proper protocols in society and business. I learned this from personal experience.

When I was a young woman in my twenties, I lived in Tokyo. My friends introduced me to their friend Saeko-san, the proprietor of *Kazehana*, a small neighborhood bar. It was an intimate place. I sometimes went there to have home-cooked Japanese dishes in the family-like environment. There was one bar, the counter shaped in a J, with just six seats. The proprietor, Saeko-san, sat in her wheelchair serving the clients. The clients were regulars and soon got to know each other. I was living alone in a small apartment, and this became my go-to place when I wanted company and a bite to eat. I also knew that I was safe and accepted there as a friend.

When my mother came to visit me, I was excited to show her my life in Tokyo.

Because I'd been living abroad, I hadn't seen her for eight years.

I took her to this favorite local oasis for a traditional Japanese dinner and a Sapporo beer. Saeko-san spoke English very well, so my mother had someone to talk to. I was chatting in Japanese to an older gentleman who had just published a new book. He had the books with him and gifted my mother and I a copy. With proper etiquette, we exchanged business cards. At that time, people did not have mobile phones and since I ran my own business, my card had only my home office phone number on it. We said our goodbyes and left.

About a week later, at eleven o'clock at night I received a phone call from that author. He wanted me to meet him and I could tell he had been drinking. I chastised him for calling me late at night and that it was improper to call me for personal reasons. I had given him my card in good faith for business reasons only. I asked him not to call me again.

This experience rattled me, because it is very out of character according to Japanese society and proper protocol. I went down to Saeko's place so she could counsel me, since that was where I had met him.

She queried me about the situation and asked me to look around and see if he was there. I didn't really recall what he looked like and replied I didn't think he was there.

Saeko-san then proceeded to ask how I felt. All the seats were taken and the Japanese clientele listened to my story and our conversation without saying anything and politely did not look directly at me so I would not be embarrassed. I was able to speak freely about I how I felt invaded in my private space in my home with the phone call, how it truly surprised me, and how I had only given my card to him because he gave me his card with his book, and after all, I was there with my mother. It would be ludicrous to think that it was anything but a professional relationship.

After a while, she told me that I did nothing wrong, but rather the author had overstepped boundaries and that was surely not acceptable behavior. She also said that I was right in coming directly there to tell her. At the other end of the bar there was a coin payphone on the bar counter, and the man who had been seated there scurried away with his head down.

The young man sitting next to me whispered, "That was him" and I gasped, "Oh, no! And I said all those things in front of him. I am so embarrassed." He replied, "No, you should not be embarrassed. He is the one who is wrong and should be ashamed."

Sacko-san had been drawing out my story on purpose so that the author could hear how it affected me. He saved face because I did not realize he was there. And he was taught a lesson by Sacko-san. What a brilliant role she played.

Points to Remember on Humility and Self-Promotion

- Some cultures value self-promotion, while others think humility is key.

- When humility is valued, have someone else sing your praises.

- Submit a written biographical introduction if self-promotion is needed.

- Observe others.

- Learn how to politely decline.

- Know that a *no* may just be a *yes* in the waiting. Offer again.

- In some cultures, criticism is taken as praise, but in others it is avoided at all costs.

- Using a go-between is common practice.

LESSON 10:

Low-Context vs. High-Context Cultures

D oing business is about communicating with others. The way people communicate their thoughts, opinions, and desires varies according to whether they are from a high- or low-context culture.

People of different cultures communicate and act in different ways according to their values and their beliefs. Low-context societies communicate what they expect explicitly. They say what they mean and do so directly. In business they value facts, figures, and direct candor.

In a high-context culture, most of the information is left unsaid, and cues are given in a subtle manner through implication. High-context cultures are prevalent in countries where the cultural demographics don't vary widely, such as in Japan and China, and where there is a strong sense of history and tradition, such as in Russia and Saudi Arabia. The unchanging culture solidifies rules and expectations throughout time.

Conscious Communications—Start with Knowing Yourself

People learn and take in information in different ways. We speak depending upon who we are addressing, what environment we are in, what the situation is, what the subject matter is, and who's within hearing range.

We are all unique. We can remember this and embrace our differences.

When I know myself, I am better able to see these differences, and therefore communicate and listen more effectively.

How are your acquaintances? Take some time to notice these different styles in your own friends, family, and professional relationships.

Low-context cultures send unambiguous messages. You see what you get, time is of the essence. They are more straightforward, and have transaction-oriented business meetings.

The U.S., Canada, Germany, Switzerland, and Fenno-Scandinavian countries are of this orientation. They think that high-context countries do not respect deadlines.

Think about management in the U.S. It is about how fast you can do it, what's the profit margin, and hopefully, is it legal?

On the other hand, high-context cultures rely more on nonverbal communication, indirect verbal signals, and implicit meanings.

In high-context cultures, developing trust is critical before any business can be done. Russia and Belarus are very high-context cultures. Relationships take time to develop trust. China, Japan, Korea, Spain, Greece, Turkey, the entire Arab world, Latin America, and Africa have this orientation. This is a lot of places to write off business from if you do not understand high-context culture. They think that low-context countries are too brash and impatient. How are you perceived?

High-context is not the average business style in American culture. However, we use it a lot in personal relationships.

How direct are you in your requests? Expressing your needs? Do you use a different context in your business and personal relationships?

Remember: *Nothing is wrong or right*. It is just a matter of getting to know yourself.

Seeing yourself clearly requires being objective. Objectivity happens when we are relaxed and accepting of reality. How objective are you?

Be Open

One way I have worked with communications is to access the body-mind field.

For example, when I feel stress, my mind is like a filter distorting reality, and then doubts and little fears crop up. I *imagine* that what's not working and the way I respond to it will never change, and what I do want will be compromised.

When I am relaxed and at peace with myself and the world around me, I can cross over in my mind into a place of being totally present and "in the moment." I listen better and I communicate more clearly and joyfully. Awareness brings relaxation. The practice of yoga is to look within and to uncover the light within. When the body and mind are in complete synergy, it brings out the spirit, the heart, the joy.

Know yourself. Which way do you communicate? Is this your preference? How do you like others to communicate with you?

When I know myself, I am more open to others. When I am relaxed, I am more attuned. This helps me to relate better to others who communicate differently, honoring each other in our diversity.

I continue to learn how to bridge communication style differences. I check in on myself: How am I feeling right now in my body-mind field? Am I under stress, apprehensive, locked into a narrow frame of mind, focused on only my needs and wants?

Respectful communications require open mindedness and an open heart. And that begins within ourselves.

LESSON 11

Hierarchy, Social Position, and Family

Cultures can be hierarchical or egalitarian. Their views on social status and family influence how they do business. This orientation is also affected by whether a culture values subjectivity over objectivity, or vice versa, or uses situational- or rule-based approaches when doing business.

In some cultures, social position is very important. It determines how people communicate and act. In an egalitarian culture, a person's social position is just seen as a framework used to achieve company goals efficiently. But in a hierarchical society, someone's position can call for submission and deep respect.

In some hierarchical cultures, taking short-cuts to talk to someone directly at the top of the hierarchy is unacceptable. You have to go through the hierarchy, one level at a time. There's a specific protocol, an order, with set rules about who you can talk to, how and when.

In Japan there is a system, and rules are followed. Even if there are no cars within view on an entire street, if the "Do Not Walk" sign is lit, everyone will wait patiently curbside until the signal changes.

Even in a culture that's not hierarchically-oriented, there can still be protocols about who you should and should not talk to for the sake of dividing labor and creating a flow in corporate communication. However, it is still acceptable for someone of a lower position to communicate with someone of a higher position, although it might not be the most practical.

In hierarchical cultures, status and power depend on how many years one has been in the company, their age, and gender. To be very simplistic, a senior executive would typically be a male with minimum thirty years in the company and over the age of sixty.

In an egalitarian society, a person's position and status are based on their merit and accomplishments. Changes in status can happen. Everyone has the same potential, and career mobility depends on the individual's proven abilities and effectiveness coupled with business needs.

One does not necessarily have to be older, more experienced, or male to be the leader.

Objective and Subjective Cultures

Overlying this pattern of hierarchy and egalitarian orientation is another perspective—whether a society is subjective or objective and whether it is situational or rule-based.

For example, in some cultures, rules are very clear. If a rule is broken, the consequences are the same for everyone, regardless of their relationship with their superiors or team.

In other societies that are situation-based or more subjective, if rules are broken, the individual's circumstances are taken into consideration.

American culture is rule-based. We have policies in place, and everyone is supposedly treated the same if a line is overstepped. There's a clear right and wrong. However, when hiring somebody to fill a position, subjective perspectives come into play. What is the circumstance, and what's needed? Someone's personality is considered as well as their skills.

How will they meld into the team? One candidate may win over another because they are assessed as a "good fit."

Be Mindful of the Hierarchy

When I was conducting training seminars in Japan, I was mindful to respect the elders, honor the hierarchy, and make sure no one lost face. I had everyone sit in rows, in hierarchical order, rather than in a circle.

First, I always chose a very simple question in English which I knew was at the conversational ability of the most senior person. The most senior person was recognized first, and able to deliver the answer correctly. This opened the way for others to speak up.

The tone was set, and now I could ask more difficult questions of the more fluent English speakers. If I had not done this, no one would have spoken up.

When there's a respected person in the room, he or she always leaves first. As a university professor in Japan, when the bell rang, no one moved until I had finished speaking, packed my briefcase and left the room.

Needless to say, when I was in the U.S. university environment and the bell rang, everyone got up even when I was mid-sentence, and I was left behind to pack up and erase my own blackboard.

In India and other Asian cultures, elders and teachers are highly respected and obeyed.

In Arab villages, there is a hierarchy depending on genealogy.

There are some charity-oriented connections, but generally the Arabs don't go outside their own circle. For example, my female colleague who lived in the Middle East told me of a gathering of two families. Both had wealth, but one had a lineage from the king and the other, although now rich, were from the ancient camel family. They would occasionally gather to eat, however the conversations stayed polite and simple with general questions such as "How are you? How is your family? How are your children?" But they never went much deeper than that.

Nepotism is common in business. Many people are related. People are appointed based on character and personality, not on their qualifications or skills. Among the Arab countries, there are varying degrees of nepotism.

Business is often done behind closed doors. They have a different view about transparency. Nontransparency is not necessarily bad. It is their way, and it works for them.

I suggest you look at the whole picture instead of focusing on one piece which is different from your way of doing things. See all of the parts and how they work together. Expand your view.

Nepotism in Spain

In Spain, when you are a friend of a friend, you are a friend. For better or worse, if you know someone, you have your foot in the door. Nepotism is alive and well in Spain, both in the political realm and business.

I asked one of my Spanish business associates about this and his response was, "Well, what did you think? Nepotism is a Latin word. The word was created because the practice existed."

Nepotism is from the Italian word nepotismo, from *nepote* "nephew," from Latin nepotem (nominative *nepos*) "grandson, nephew."

Developing relationships is important in Spain. People will first give business to someone they know, directly or indirectly, even if it is not at the best price.

Jobs are often given to people just because they are related to a friend of a friend, not necessarily because they're the best suited for the position.

This pervades all of Spanish society, from business, to university and government positions.

Family Before Work or Work Before Family

A Spanish businessman in customer sales complained to me that sometimes Spaniards do not pay their invoices on time, finding this an acceptable reason: "I have to take care of my family first—then I will pay you."

In the Spanish culture, family is family and the Sunday dinner, celebrations, or frequent gatherings include everybody.

As an American businessperson, know when to schedule meetings in Spain, Italy and many other countries. Most Europeans value their weekends and holiday time to be with family and will not work then.

Points to Remember: Business Style Considerations

- In egalitarian cultures, someone's position is just a framework used to achieve company goals.

- In hierarchical cultures, someone's position calls for submission and deep respect.

- In hierarchical cultures, you usually need to have experience and be of a certain age and gender to rise to the top.

- In egalitarian cultures, everyone has the same status and potential.

- In objective cultures, the same rules apply to everyone.

- Subjective cultures are more situation-based.

- Elders and teachers are highly respected in India and Asia.

- Nepotism is prevalent in Spain and Arab countries

LESSON 12

Entertaining, Etiquette, and Seating

Business entertaining, etiquette, and seating arrangements are important in many cultures. Prepare to be entertained and dine out. Seating arrangements in business meetings might also be formalized.

In China, the seat of honor is reserved for the master of the banquet or the guest with the highest status. It is in the center facing east or facing the entrance. The people of higher position sit closer to the master of the banquet. Those of lowest position sit furthest from the seat of honor, closest to the entrance.

Many restaurants in China offer private dining rooms with large round tables. Seating may not be marked, but there are unspoken rules for who sits where. If in doubt, hesitate, showing humility, and wait until you are told where to sit.

Seating etiquette is also followed in business meetings in China and Japan.

Sometimes the lead two counterparts are in the middle of the table facing each other and on each side are the associates facing similar ranking counterparts. Interpreters are seated behind or next to their client.

Business cards are laid out on the table before each person in the same diagrammatic format.

Here are two diagrams that show seating for business meetings in China.

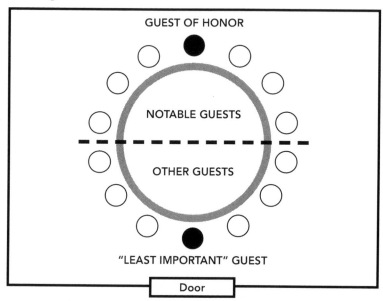

Seating etiquette for a business banquet in China.

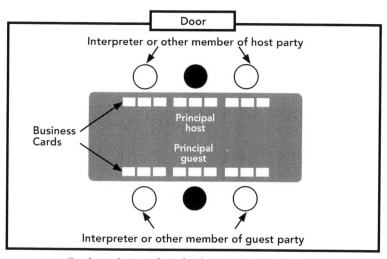

Seating etiquette for a business meeting in China.

The Long Wait to Eat in Beijing

My Chinese-speaking American colleague Matt told me a story of when his parents visited him in Beijing and they went to dinner with Chinese friends and other American expatriates. After an hour-and-a-half to get across Beijing, they were already tired and hungry. Then it took a lot of time to decide what to order because there are many courses in the meal and each has to be balanced not only nutritionally but also energetically.

His parents were not only the eldest at the table, but also the guests of honor, and so they were placed farthest from the door, facing the kitchen. His mother was talking on and on, but no one would touch the food. Finally, Matt had to say, "Mother stop talking, pick up your chopsticks, and just touch the food with them." Immediately everyone else dived into an eating frenzy.

No one can start eating before the honored guest has touched the food.

There is seating protocol, formal toasts, many courses in the meal, and considerations about how to balance them.

In the U.S. we also have protocols. In a restaurant, we wait until everyone has been served or give verbal permission to someone to go ahead and start. In the home, we wait for the hostess of the house to pick up her fork first.

From Invitation to Obligation

Accepting an invitation to dinner can incur an obligation. Inviting someone to dinner is also a way of returning a favor.

The Chinese can be opportunistic. You may be invited to lunch and wonder, "Why? What does he want?" Invitations are a form of developing relationships and relationships come with mutual favors. Be observant of the conversation points. There may be mention about someone who wants to go to the U.S. to study and needs a recommendation letter, or a hint might come up about something else.

It is acceptable to refuse invitations politely with excuses such as, "I'm too busy," "You're too busy," or "I don't want to inconvenience you." But the Chinese like the challenge and will keep asking. Then you might finally accept. But you can just keep being polite and extending the noncommitment longer.

In the Middle East, do not refuse an invitation overtly. But it is acceptable to delay and put it off.

Give a reason, such as "I'm busy now." They will keep asking and you can still put it off. *Sometimes you may need to be selective in your acceptances.* To have a Western acquaintance is cause to show off and be the talk of the town.

At the end of a meal, Uzbek Muslims bring their hands together in a "prayer" position in front of the chest, then raise them together to trace an invisible circle, and return them open to face level while saying "omīn" (amen; so be it; truly), and then wipe their face.

Two Uzbek school teachers teach me the non-verbal gestures to give thanks after a meal.

Cucumber Sandwiches in Japan

At times, you may not find what you normally eat. Taste new foods. And, sometimes you just have to have what you want.

I was the only interpreter for ABC News at the Tokyo Economic Summit in 1979 for a staff of fifty guys from New York City and Los Angeles, including anchors Peter Jennings and Sam Donaldson. I had quite the job. When not on location reporting that "The President has no comment at this time," the ABC news crew utilized my Japanese language skills, local knowledge, and connections for off-site stories.

My own native culture know-how came in handy. Although very nicely arranged, do you really think that these all-American guys would be satisfied eating the catered Japanese cucumber finger sandwiches? No way. "We want meat, burgers, fries, and ice cream." OK. I found them. Fortunately, it was Tokyo and I could get them everything they wanted in the first Japanese McDonald's that had opened just a few years earlier.

Reading a Nonverbal Business Signal in Japan

As a Japanese-speaking U.S. citizen living in Tokyo in the 1970s, I found that U.S. executives and business people preferred a non-Japanese national as their business interpreter. There was often a lack of trust between what was said and how it was translated.

I was able to assist beyond the call of translating. The Hanes Senior VP of Marketing contracted me for the week of a U.S. Department of Commerce Boutique America in Tokyo. I presented myself as a Hanes company team member instead of a temporary local consultant, which would hold more status for the Japanese. By reading cultural signals, I was able to point out which Japanese contacts were interested in doing business with Hanes and which ones were not.

For example, we were wined and dined, yet I noticed that even though the Hanes Senior VP was the guest, there was no Japanese counterpart at his same level. This meant we were being socially entertained as foreign guests, but that business was not going any further.

As the visitor, you may be treated with politeness and hospitality. But if you are of a higher status than the staff who are in the meeting or taking you out, that is a sign that's saying, "There's no business happening here."

By picking up this cultural signal, we could avoid wasting any more time with them afterwards and moved on to other perspective business partners instead. This is a cross-cultural point you may not understand or even look at.

What to Note When Assessing Business Meals in Asia

- Who is at the meeting or meal?
- Who in the meeting is representing the other side?
- Who is the go-between?
- How much has happened beforehand in this business connection?

Other Points to Remember

- If unsure where to sit, wait until you are told.
- In China, no one eats before the honored guest has touched the food.
- An invitation can turn into an obligation.

LESSON 13

Personal Space, Eye Contact, and Touch

When you are unaware of your nonverbal communications, you might inadvertently offend someone or make them uncomfortable. You can misunderstand someone else's nonverbals, too.

Nonverbal communication happens all the time, whether you intend it or not.

There are several categories of nonverbal communication. Nonverbal communication involves the use of personal space, touch, body movements, gestures and facial expressions, eye movement, use of time, and vocal features. It is important to know the differences across cultures. What is considered acceptable in one culture may not be acceptable in another.

For example, Germany, Norway, and the U.S. have more cool and decisive business cultures. Maintaining personal space is important, and they do not engage in much ritual. Touch among strangers is limited to a handshake, and eye contact is expected.

While in Brazil, Italy, and Mexico, the culture is warm and impulsive and physical touch such as cheek-kissing, hugging, and touching during conversation are common in business interactions. Too much eye contact, however, can be seen as confrontational.

In contrast, the Japanese and Chinese cultures are accommodating and nonconfrontational with more ritual, respect and no touch. Eye contact can be uncomfortable.

Personal Space

Personal space describes the immediate empty space surrounding a person. The amount of personal space considered "comfortable" is variable and subjective. Different cultures have different norms for how close they stand or sit. When people are speaking, the degree of intimacy or remoteness of the relationship is determined by the spatial arrangements or variations in distance between people talking.

Personal space is an emotional as well as physical space.

Changes in personal space can reflect a conscious or unconscious desire to connect or create more distance. Individuals within the same culture may also have slightly different behaviors due to their personal comfort levels.

How far apart do you stand when you are in conversation? How far apart do you stand when you are in line in a store or for public transportation?

In business, the use of personal space is influenced by someone's social distinction or status. For example, colleagues of equal status may stand closer together, yet when one colleague is of lesser rank, he or she will stand further away from the person of higher rank. The personal distance maintained between men and men and women and women in most cultures differs as well, with the greatest distinction being a formal distance between men and women, even if they are of equal status.

We also make unintentional shifts in personal space. For example, if the speaker's voice becomes louder or the pitch becomes higher, the listener might move backwards a bit.

Personal Space and Proximity Considerations

- Is this an intimate distance for embracing, touching, or whispering?
- Is this a social distance for acquaintances?
- Is this a public distance for strangers?
- What is the setting?
- Who is directly interacting? Who is nearby and observing the interaction?
- What is the culture of the participants in conversation?

Eye Contact

Eye contact is often unconsciously used as a means of nonverbal communication.

Someone thinking visually might physically turn their eyes away, to more easily visualize and access their imagination.

Someone whose thinking is connected to what they are hearing might turn their eyes as much as possible to one of their ears. (But looking side to side could be understood as a sign of lying.) Someone thinking with their physical feelings might look downwards, connecting to the body where emotions are easily felt.

In the U.S., eye contact shows you are interested and engaged in the conversation. Eyes are the central point of focus. Wandering eyes or looking elsewhere may be considered insulting, or at least a sign of disinterest, or distraction.

In more formal circumstances—for example a job interview—strong eye contact can be taken as a sign of confidence, while a lack of it can be seen as a lack of confidence.

We often base relationships on the emotions generated from eye contact, so be aware.

Eye Contact Self-Awareness

- Do you look someone directly into the eyes when speaking? When listening?
- Or do you only look sometimes, and if so, for how long?
- Is eye contact brief? Or do you hold a gaze, or even stare?
- Do your eyes move around?
- How do your eyes change with your feelings, e.g., when you are sincere or when you are hiding your real emotions?
- How do your eyes change with your physical facial expressions, e.g., when you smile or frown?

Eye Contact Across Cultures

When your eyes are up, are you thinking? Recalling a memory? Showing boredom? What if you add your head into the mix and lower the head while looking upwards, which can be a coy, suggestive action?

In some cultures, looking down—avoiding eye contact—can be a sign of submission, fear or even guilt, while in others it is a sign of respect.

A lack of blinking in one culture could indicate interest, but in other cultures it can be aggressive, affectionate, or deceptive.

Glancing can show a true desire, like looking at a door (wanting to leave) or at a class of water (when thirsty). If a person is interested in someone, their eyes will follow.

Closing the eyes allows us to go inside and shut out the world. It can be a reaction to fear or embarrassment, or in some cultures it is a way to "go within" and reflect upon something more sincerely.

"Look at me when I am speaking to you," is a common parental command during a serious conversation with a child in the U.S.

Here, we like eye contact. Sometimes in moments of reflection or thinking, the eyes can look elsewhere, briefly, but eye contact is expected when greeting, speaking, and listening—in fact, most of the time. This is the same in the UK, Australia, and most of Europe.

In Arab countries eye contact connects people. Long, strong eye contact is often a method to show sincerity as if saying, "I am telling you the truth."

However, there are strict gender rules. Too much eye contact can be misconstrued as a romantic overture. Limit or avoid eye contact between women and men.

In China and Japan, which are hierarchical cultures, direct eye contact is often considered inappropriate. Subordinates should not make steady eye contact with their superiors, as it is considered disrespectful. Looking inward or downward shows humility. Or it shows the person is in thought, considering what you are saying. That being said, children are indulged and often stare at foreigners.

Latin American and African cultures are all distinct, but most are hierarchical.

Therefore, in many situations intense eye contact could be interpreted as confrontational, aggressive, and extremely disrespectful.

That being said, in Russia during a Vodka toast hold your gaze until you see the bottoms up, or it is an insult.

Touch

There are many types of touch. Here are a few:

- Professional or functional task orientation
- Social, polite, ritualistic interaction
- Friendship, warmth
- Love, intimacy, emotional attachment

People have differing levels of comfort with touch in professional settings. Some wish for more, while others do not want any. Women usually touch other women more often than women and men touch one another.

In one culture, a hand on the shoulder by the manager may mean a supportive gesture. However, in another culture, the gesture can be seen as a sexual advance.

The person in power is more likely to touch a subordinate, but the subordinate should not touch back. This can lead to confusion.

A weak handshake can be uncomfortable. And, when a handshake is held too long, the nonverbal gesture can interrupt the verbal communication taking place because of the increased awareness of touch.

Also, for some, the handshake is avoided altogether because there is an aversion to touch, and especially to perspiring (sweaty) palms.

A Brazilian female client of mine, an engineer in her twenties, was recently relocated to Ohio. I was her trainer and cross-cultural business coach to help her integrate into the U.S. She said, "I really miss coming into work and being able to hug and kiss my colleagues as we begin and end our day. I am used to communicating with a touch on the arm or pat on the back. Here in the U.S. we are not allowed to touch in the workplace."

Even in one's own culture, touch carries an individual comfort level. I was once at a Chamber of Commerce meeting in Cleveland, Ohio, when a male high school acquaintance— someone I had not seen in twenty-five years and not a close friend— came over and greeted me with a kiss on the cheek. I thought it was highly inappropriate, and sent a private message publically. He was probably not aware of this, and his happiness in seeing me most likely diminished when I took him aside and told him never to do that again, especially in a business setting in the Midwest. Maybe my years of Japanese appropriateness and separation of public and private face came into play. Maybe it was just shock. Whatever the reason, my U.S. individualistic, low-context communication stood out with the directness of my reprimand.

The day Violeta, a new friend at the University of Sevilla, and I discussed renting the apartment room together, we were walking downtown after school. One custom in Spain is to *pasear*, or stroll around downtown restaurant/bar-hopping, sampling different kinds of *tapas* (snacks). Foods from other cultures can be appetizing or not. I tried everything. This was the first time I saw ham hocks hanging from the ceiling, dried blood cakes, and *calamares* (fried squid), all very strange to me.

Violeta linked her arm into mine to walk together more intimately. My first instinct was one of surprise and awkwardness, since in Ohio, I had never walked arm-in-arm with another woman.

Then it occurred to me that this was a Spanish custom. I took a deep breath, and didn't miss a step as we strolled arm-in-arm around downtown Sevilla. Later I noticed other women doing the same.

By opening into my acculturation and experiencing this simple but new custom made me feel I was becoming a part of Spain and I was happy to have a new friend who was treating me just like any other. I was being accepted and integrated, not seen as just the American foreigner.

TIP: Observe Others

If you are comfortable, join in the local customs. When you incorporate these simple customs in the culture you are in, it will not only make you feel more integrated, but also elicit that response of inclusion from others

However, if you are uncomfortable, honor that within yourself. There is no need to be anyone different than who you are.

Once, at a bullfight, the bull's ear was cut off and thrown to the spectators and landed at my feet. "Take it home to America," my friends said. Hmmm. No, thank you! Not remotely within my comfort zone.

When you are learning what is acceptable touch, observe others in that culture.

Physical Touch Observations

- How close are the participants standing? Are they outside of or within body contact distance?

- Are they touching at all?

- If so, what parts of the body are in contact? Hands, as in a handshake? Air-kissing with cheeks touching? Pat on the back or touch on the arm? Full or partial upper body hug?

- How long are they in physical touch? Is it a short gesture? A prolonged contact?

LESSON 14

Verbal vs. Nonverbal Cues

People gain meaning in communication based on cultural references. If you do not understand or know these, you will not be able to communicate fully, even if you speak the language fluently.

When children are learning a certain language, they are also learning the nonverbal idiosyncrasies (beyond personal space and touch) at the same time. This nonverbal communication becomes almost unconscious in later years as language takes precedent, especially in low-context cultures.

We are oblivious to the nonverbal elements in our own culture, and assume other cultures communicate in the same way. This can cause misunderstandings and misinterpretations in cross-cultural communications.

While trying to become a part of the society on a daily basis, you might always be considered an outsider, an alien. Different cultures will respond differently to your uniqueness. Spain, for example, is embracing. Japan is closed. Even the Japanese word for "foreigner" is comprised of the pictogram characters meaning outside person.

Tone of Voice

Voice does not always have the same interpretation across cultures.

For example, when I speak Japanese, my voice rises to a more feminine pitch, much like Japanese women speak. This is natural in that culture. Japanese employs both male and female language, which adds to the pitch differences.

However, that same raised pitch can be seen as sexist to other cultures like Americans. Why would a woman lift her voice to a high pitch, a feminine stereotypical ploy?

On the other hand, consider how American English is seen by Russians. American intonation and voice tone has more expressiveness and variation than Russian, for example.

My Belarussian friend called it the "Barbie voice": "OH! How WONderful!" (emphasized and raised pitch). She said it seemed fake. Enthusiasm expressed in this way sounds insincere to those whose native nonverbals do not include a wide variety of pitch.

In perspective, this is what the high-pitched Japanese voice tone seems like to an American. It all depends upon where you are coming from.

Whether you are socially traveling or on business, nonverbal communication is key to understanding what is said beyond verbal words.

To communicate and comprehend nonverbally requires

awareness, observation and openness. You have to think beyond the words, outside the box, and get into a creative mode.

Nonverbal Communication Anecdotes

Nonverbal communication can feel childlike, like a fun game of imagination. And it can be easy.

Imagine you are in a store. Obviously, you might want to buy something. Point at the item. Look at the price tag. If there is none, then the merchant will use his hands and fingers to indicate the price. You smile or frown at it, shake your head, make a gesture raising your hand and then lowering it to indicate lowering the price, re-gesture the numbers with your counting fingers, and so on. If you want less quantity or a smaller size, you can indicate this with having your hands facing each other and drawing them together—or more quantity and a larger size by pulling them apart. You do not need a translator.

Of course, if all you want is the cheapest price, then you could take a native speaker or a translator with you who knows the value of the goods. Yes, I know it is unfair in a Westerner's view to be charged more than the locals. But if you want to have an experience of your own, it can be worth it. Then again, you may be surprised by the vendor giving you a little something extra free of charge to be friendly.

In a small village market in Kyrgyzstan, there were no other foreigners in the entire village. A group of women gave me free fruit and walnuts from several outdoor stands. They all pitched in to welcome the stranger. My "Thank you" in Kyrgyz and Russian made them laugh. The smiles were precious. The moment is remembered, still.

Multicultures of women in the marketplace on cellphones selling tandoor oven-baked naan *(leavened flatbread.)*

Anywhere in the world, imagine you are asking directions. You approach a safe-looking person. Make sure they do not seem to be in a rush. As a woman, I always approach another woman.

Point at a map, if you have one, or say one word which you have looked up in your travel dictionary, or even use the phrase "Where is the post office?" in their language. If you botch the phrase, don't worry. You have made a connection. You are a visitor in their country and they will respond. You can just shrug your shoulders and look confused without saying anything.

They will usually be delighted to help, or maybe turn away if they worry their English is not good enough to help you. More likely than not, however, they might not only point to your map, show you where you are and where you are going, but also even walk you part of the way or practice English with you.

Now you have a little experience to remember for this day, this place. Sometimes you may find a fluent English speaker or someone who wants to practice their English more, and they will want to spend more time with you.

Questions You Are Asked May Surprise You

I once asked directions to a woman in Bishkek. She was of a minority group, the Uyghur. She spoke reasonable English and wanted to practice it. So, I invited her to walk with me. She told me about the Uyghur people and culture during our walk and, in another surprising revelation, asked, "Why do American women not want to dress pretty?" She was referring to my shoes. No way was I walking in high heels if I were not dressed for business, and so I replied as candidly as she had asked me the question: "I dress for comfort when I have to walk a lot, but in my culture we do not think comfortable shoes are manly."

Sometimes the kinds of questions you are asked can give you insight into the culture. Frequently I was asked, "Why do you not have children?" I tried many different answers before finding one that seemed logical to the Central Asians.

"I did not marry until later in life." (That did not seem reason enough.)

"When I was younger, I concentrated on my education and career first." (Again, no reason.)

"In my culture, it is common for women not to have children." (Again, falls on deaf ears.)

"I am a teacher and my students of all ages are my children." (This one worked!) So I memorized it in Russian and used it frequently.

Mental Filters and Stereotyping Attitudes

Once in the countryside of Japan, I asked some young women for directions.

They were so in shock that a blonde blue-eyed American was speaking fluent Japanese that they stared at my hair and eyes and responded back, "You speak Japanese!" They just stared and repeated it, never answering my question.

Another time on a local commuter train into Tokyo, a young child stared at my eyes while saying to his mother "She has long legs!" The stereotype of a Westerner is long legs and the child knew this, but just fixated on my round blue eyes. *Kami no ke ga chigau* is a Japanese expression which literally translates as "Your hair is different" but means "You are an alien."

Saying one thing and indicating another is a clue to how we use nonverbal communication. The young women I had encountered were nonverbally saying, "I cannot believe it. Your Japanese is fluent but you do not look Japanese at all. How can this be? I am blown away and cannot even answer your question about directions." The child was saying, "My gosh, Mommy, there is an alien over there and I have heard they have long legs but I am shocked to see blue eyes too."

Finding Shelter in Turkey

When some friends and I traveled Marco Polo's Silk Route, we drove near Mount Ararat in Turkey, where Noah's Ark is said to have come to rest. We were a motley group of four: an elderly Japanese professor, two Spaniards, and me. It was a very remote area. A group of indigenous mountain folk had laid boulders in the single lane road to stop us. We did not want to be detained in a strange terrain, so we continued on cautiously weaving around the obstacles.

It was starting to get dark, and for hours we had not seen any town or villages. We came into a valley with a large plain and an open field with a house on the hill. This was our best bet to rest for the night; the rough mountain road was too dangerous to maneuver in the dark.

We walked to the house and a Turkish man and woman with baby greeted us. We then gestured, one, two, three, four pointing to each of our group members, and then tilting our heads to the side with palms together resting on one cheek (to indicate sleep); we were asking if there was a place we could spend the night.

Accommodatingly, the man gestured for us to follow him. He took us into the field and used the same gestures—one, two, three, four—rested his tilted head on his hands, and then pointed to a platform up in a tree right in the middle of the field.

They brought out a folding table and chairs and some grapes and bread. We gestured to pay them, but they shook their heads, "no." Instead, the man gestured to the cap one of my companions was wearing, who immediately took it off and gave it to the Turkish man. Then the Turkish man gave his own cap to my companion. We had made a connection. The gesture of food was because we were guests. The cap exchange was a bridge both parties crossed to exchange something as a keepsake.

With a Japanese-German dictionary, a few words, and a lot of gestures, we got to know each other. He knew a smattering of German, as he worked in a factory in Germany ten months out of the year and was home now to be with his family. We showed each other coins and monies from Spain, Germany, the U.S., Japan, and Turkey and played the money game of seeing the values of each by making stacks of coins and looking at the numbers on the coins.

It was just a nonverbal communication. Everyone knows about money, but no money was ever exchanged or given. It was a social interaction, not a business transaction.

We slept well on the tree house platform, up from the ground where who knows what might roam, on our fluffy pillows in sleeping bags. But much to my surprise, when I opened my eyes, two Turkish men, friends of our host, were on the ladder just staring at us. I nudged the others and said, "Let's go. I think they want our fluffy pillows."

Looking back, I think they just were in awe of the group of us: a Japanese, two Spaniards, and an American traveling the world.

We journeyed on, spending a month in Iran, another in Afghanistan, and then crossed through the Khyber Pass into Pakistan. We read the only English newspaper pasted up in the central plaza saying, "Smallpox epidemic." So, while we waited until morning to quickly cross into India, I holed out in a pension room above a tea house, while my traveling companion went to get us some food. The first floor tea house was all men and it was huge, perhaps hosting one hundred people or more. I did not want to pass in and out of it too many times.

In my room there was one window facing the window of another building. I looked out. There was a woman in the other window. She looked at me. It felt like a communication was already happening.

A wave from me. A wave from her. A gesture from her, pointing to me and a beckoning hand, for me to come there. She gestured holding an invisible teacup in her hands and lifting it up and down to her mouth. A split second thought came into my mind of "No way I am leaving to go to a stranger's house. I can just imagine a male family member coming home and who knows what would happen."

So I gestured back to her the same, inviting her to come here to drink tea with me. She responded with gestures of shaking her head "No," pointing to her chest, stroking her chin, and waving her index finger back and forth and then repeating the invitation back to me.

I used the same gestures back indicating, "No, my man will not let me go there, but you should come here to drink tea." At a stalemate, we both just shrugged our shoulders, accepting our situation. We continued to stare at each other with a desire to connect further, yet content to have had this powerful nonverbal exchange, beyond language, across different socio-economic classes, transcending cultures, and into the heart. I could feel it and I know she did, too.

I wish I knew her name. But I will never forget her essence of openness to reach out and invite me in.

It only takes about 500 words in a language to be able to hold a simple conversation. Hand gestures, facial expressions, distance between people while talking, eye contact or not, silent pauses, position of the arms, can fill in the gaps.

TIP: Watch Your Hand Gestures

It is easy to offend when you use the wrong hand gestures.

The OK sign is not OK everywhere. Neither is the Peace sign, index and middle fingers extended.

Two American college girls sitting at a sidewalk café in Spain was a rarity at the time I was living there. Having strangers coming up to us asking questions was new to me, and all too frequent. It bothered me. Can't I just have a cup of coffee, alone with my girlfriend? No privacy.

So after a short exchange, I would say "Go away!" (ivayase!), and yet I mistakenly used the American hand gesture, with my fingers down, flipping my hand back and forth, trying to shoo them away. I tried again and again. But these young men would not move. They just chuckled and chuckled.

Finally, I realized that gesture actually meant "come here." Talk about mixed signals!

A Japanese Maneki-Neko, or "Hello Cat," appears to Westerners to be waving, but the gesture is understood as one of beckoning in Japan.

A Japanese maneki-neko (the term means "beckoning cat") is often displayed at the entrances of restaurants and shops. It is popularly called "hello cat" by most, but not all, Westerners, because the gesture the cat seems to be making is a side-to-side wave. But it is actually a flicking of the fingers up and down. In Japan, Italy and Spain, this gesture means "come here" as illustrated in the story above.

TIP: In business negotiations, speak your native language or have an interpreter.

In business, be sure you have a translator, mentor, or colleagues to help you. In business we cannot afford to insult a potential connection. We need to bridge the communication and cultural gaps with skills that ensure a growing future relationship.

Laugh and Learn

In social settings, using less-than-perfect language can be a plus to bridging and deepening relationships. Before you travel anywhere, at least learn to say hello, goodbye, and thank you, and other simple phrases you believe may be useful. This shows you are interested in the people and their language, and makes them more willing to enter into conversation with you.

Be ready for some laughter. Mistakes can and do happen. And that too becomes a new conversation piece.

In my learning stage in Spain, I thought I was using the phrase "I am embarrassed," about my limited Spanish-speaking ability. I would say, *"Estoy embarazada,"* but oops, it turns out that means, "I am pregnant." As it was obviously untrue, the laughter elicited was full-scale.

Learn What is Offensive and Avoid It

In Russia, when in a crowded theatre or concert and you need to pass the people seated in your row, do so facing them, not with your behind to them. This is the opposite of how people maneuver such situations in the U.S.

In the Middle East, do not fully cross your legs and show the bottom of your shoes. It is a grave insult.

In Thailand and Burma, strict Buddhist countries, do not pat children on the head. The head is where they believe the soul enters and leaves the body and it is a sacred spot.

Sometimes you may feel very uncomfortable with a particular custom. Notice what others do and try to follow it.

When I was in Spain, *piropos*, public compliments to women as they walk by, were common: constant shouts from workers on the street of, "Hey, blonde one," or "pretty girl," to me were uncomfortable, since in my culture they seemed at best strange, and at worst, harassing. And they were not uniquely said for me, but every woman walking by. Even a woman with three children in tow received the comment, "You are more beautiful than the Virgin Mary." I observed that women just ignored them, so I did the same.

LESSON 15

It's About Time

Cultures view and value time differently. This impacts our communications. Time can be viewed in regards to achieving goals and completing tasks. Time can also be viewed in regards to balancing and nurturing relationships.

People structure, manage, and respond to time differently. Time perceptions affect punctuality, willingness to wait, speed of speech, and degree of patience in listening.

Chronemics is the study of the role of time in communications. Cultures and individuals can be considered as monochronic or polychronic.

Monochronic Cultures

In monochronic time orientation, actions are divided into specific, precise steps and done one at a time. Time is managed, arranged, and scheduled.

Germany, Austria and Switzerland are some of the most highly monochronic cultures. Most of the U.S. is monochronic. Other monochronic cultures include the UK, Canada, Scandinavia, South Korea, Taiwan, and Japan.

For Americans, time is a tangible commodity. We see this in business phrases such as, "Time is money."

- Let's buy some time.

- I'll make time for it.

- Don't waste time.

- Can we save time on that?

We buy, spend, use, make, and live in time-bound consciousness. We have schedules to follow, appointments to keep, meetings that start and end at a particular time, and quarterly objectives to achieve. Time is broken down into units of years, months, days, hours, minutes.

Many monochronic people multi-task, thinking they will save time, but they still think about time as linear.

Monochronic cultures are task-oriented and focused on getting the job done. If others do not have the same perception of time, it can cause business difficulties.

For monochronic people, arriving on time means early or exactly on time. If someone is five to ten minutes late, a call must be made to explain why. Meetings also end on time and there is usually a set agenda. If someone is late, or has a different time orientation, it is considered disrespectful. Plans are rarely changed.

In verbal communication, monochronic people will speak one at a time. They take turns. The ability to listen patiently and wait your turn is considered polite. When emotions run high, or there is a disagreement, people might interrupt each other.

Monochronic cultures tend to build more practical and even temporary relationships.

Polychronic Cultures

Polychronic time, on the other hand, is when several actions are taking place at once. Latin America, Africa, South Asia, and Arab countries share the system of polychronic time.

People from these cultures are not as focused on accounting for each and every minute. They are more concerned with tradition and relationships, and are less task-oriented. Traditional societies feel they have all the time in the world.

If they are with family or friends, they do not watch the clock, or worry about being late for another appointment. In fact, they may even schedule multiple engagements at the same time. They have a less formal perception of time and are not ruled by precise schedules.

People who are polychronic will often talk at the same time or interrupt each other frequently in normal conversation. They will also talk for longer periods of time. They may also speak in a nonlinear way, circling back to the point repeatedly.

Polychronic people will concentrate on the event around them rather than the task at hand. They will consider goals and results more seriously than deadlines and schedules. They are committed to people, relationships and shared connections more than the job and end results. Plans change more easily. They will tend to build more lifelong relationships.

Cross-Cultural Difficulties with Time in Business Relationships

You need to know how your business associates view time and be aware of your own perception of time. Low-context and individualistic cultures tend to be monochronic, while high-context and collective cultures tend to be polychronic.

Psychologically, people can be past-, present-, or future-time-oriented.

If past-oriented, they will blur the past and the present. Present-time oriented people are living for the now and have little aversion to risk. Future-oriented people are focused on the broad picture and highly goal-oriented.

In some cultures, even the language does not include the past or future tense in verbs, only the present. Tenseless languages include Burmese; Chinese; Guarani, an indigenous language of South America; Dyirbal, an Australian Aboriginal language; and Greenlandic, an Eskimo-Aleut language. In Indonesian, a word-by-word translation might be, "You yesterday come to dinner?"

Americans have a future orientation. Tomorrow is what we look towards. We like to move onto new challenges, sometimes even skipping over immediate issues.

To a polychronic person, Americans can be seen as anxious for agreement, always in a hurry. They want to resolve issues quickly with some solution being better than no solution. Polychronic people think, "We'll get there when we get there."

But there are crossovers in style. While Japan is monochronic like the U.S., and both cultures value punctuality, Japan will be very slow to come to agreement. This is because other cultural factors come into play in addition to their time orientation.

In India, time consciousness is less strict than in the U.S,
Japan, and Europe. This can be a frustrating situation for
business. I worked in a Japanese Seibu group company that
imported carpets from India. Cross-cultural views about
time were quite different and the shipments were often late.

TIP: If you are from the U.S., UK, Japan, or Germany, Breathe Deeply and Relax

You may be frustrated with the lack of time awareness in
other cultures.

The sense of time in Spain, Latin and most of South
America is more vague and less structured than in the U.S.
"How long will it take?" is a difficult question to answer. In the
business environment, meetings are not necessarily planned
with an agenda and an ending time. Relationships trump. The
meeting will end when everyone has had their say.

Imagine you are in the Canary Islands or the Philippines.
You are going to a business meeting or event. You call a
driver to pick you up.

The dialogue goes like this:

Client: Where are you now?

Driver: Near.

Client: How near?

Driver: Near.

Client: How long will it take you to come from there to
here?

Driver: Soon.

Client: How soon?

Driver: Two minutes.

And twenty minutes, not two minutes, later the car
arrives.

Time is Hard to Pinpoint

In some cultures, even if you ask questions in various ways, you still may not get a straight answer, especially if it relates to time.

In other business situations, it goes like this.

Sales Company: "When can you come?"
Client Company: "We'll call you."
Sales Company: "What do you mean?"
Client Company: "Soon. We'll call you."

Another real conversation:

Sales Rep: "You'll send me an email? When?"
Customer: "Soon."
Sales Rep: "What day?"
Customer: "Soon."

It is an avoidance of pinpointing time exactly. Timeliness is not a high priority.

Time and Power in Business

Someone's status can be indicated by their use of time. For example, a boss can interrupt an ongoing process or even call an impromptu meeting. But an average worker would have to make an appointment to see a higher-up boss. Sometimes time is used to establish a position of power, display dominance, or show status.

Consider these scenarios:

- **Amount of time you need to wait**
  - The higher the status, the more power and control.
  - The lower status person's time is considered less valuable.

- **Amount of time you have to talk in a meeting**
  - Who talks the longest?

- Who initiates and ends the conversation?
- Who asks the questions?
- Do the participants take turns and is everyone heard?
- **Control of your time at work**
  - Do you need to report your time?
  - Do you have control of your time and flexibility in your work schedule?

Know Your Holidays and When Businesses Close

Know the local holidays in the country where you are traveling.

Europeans often take vacations for the month in August. Most businesses in Japan close during late April/early May's Golden Week, the longest vacation period of the year. Two other Japanese holidays, the New Year in January and Obon Festival in August, are observed for a week. Central and South America and Latin European countries close shop during the Spring Semana Santa (Holy Week).

People doing business in Muslim countries during Ramadan often find a lower level of productivity, increased difficulty in meeting deadlines, and challenges scheduling meetings.

Also remember the midday siesta time. In Spain and some other countries, shops, restaurants, cafés close in the afternoon for several hours.

When I was in Italy, we extended our trip for a couple of days. We tried to rent a car in a village outside Florence, but the one and only location was closed because of a local holiday. Fortunately, the Italian hospitality came through. The local innkeeper knew the car rental owner and telephoned him at his home. Within a short time, we had a rental car,

and a good memory of kindnesses extended. Ask for help.
People all over the world will amaze you.

*Feria (Spring Festival) in Spain is a time of extravagant private parties
to entertain clients and solicit business connections. Here are my Spanish
nieces in Sevilla.*

LESSON 16

Women in Business

When I wrote my master's thesis in Japan, I disproved my own theory. My subject translated to English was *Sex, Status, and Second Person Pronouns: 107 Ways to Say "You" in Japanese*. I was coming from the orientation of an American woman of the 1970s in the midst of feminism. I believed the Japanese language was sexist and had a social impact on sexism in Japan at that time.

However, my blind research showed that for Japanese people themselves, male and female, young and old, urban and rural, rich and poor, the opposite was true from their cultural orientation. Rules and regulations for a hierarchical society give order and structure. It is what it is. There is no feeling about its meaning and no desire to alter it. If changed, it would be strange, awkward and well, just not *Japanese*.

One of my friends in Japan, Ryoko Ozawa, was a politician. I was able to observe her during a session of the state representatives. I was surprised to hear her shout and appear angry. It is rare for the Japanese to show emotions in a professional setting. I asked her what was happening. She replied, "I was not angry, I just needed to be heard." She could only do that by using male-style words in a loud voice. Her following comment was revealing: "And they think I am so rebellious, they are afraid of me!" She broke the societal rules, so she was more able to push through her agendas because she was out of norm. They could not ignore her as they would another woman.

I too was able to do business successfully in Japan. By speaking Japanese fluently, I was considered out of the norm, which was a benefit. I was not Japanese. I was not just a woman. I was not just an American. I was a Japanese-speaking American, a rarity—and therefore, I was seen as Harriet Russell, a person without category. I was dealt with directly as an individual. I established great trust and friendships and got my foot in the door where many other foreigners never had, not even men.

Find what makes you unique so you relate based on yourself instead of your gender.

Avoiding Inappropriate Situations

As a young single woman, I always made sure I never found myself in a situation which could be considered professionally inappropriate.

I was taken to hostess bars, but of the high-end exclusive caliber for mixed business group entertainment. And always, there was another woman, a Japanese secretary or administrative assistant from the department with us.

Hostess bars employ mostly female staff who serve drinks and sit with customers for attentive conversation and may even dance with them. There are also host bars, with male staff, who serve female customers. This is part of the nighttime entertainment in Japan and other East Asian countries. There are various levels of host/hostess bars, from high-end exclusive clubs with only corporate account clients, to common public access bars.

When we entered the establishment, one of the male colleagues would politely say, "This is our professional business associate" so that the hostess knew the relationship was business not personal and I was treated accordingly. When we left by taxi, I was taken directly home and dropped off before the other woman, so I was never alone in the company of only male counterparts. Such politeness!

I never went to a business lunch alone with just one other man, except for when I met with my mentor. Otherwise, it was always with two colleagues or a group.

One day, however, I found out that Ms. Ozawa (the politician I mentioned earlier) knew someone in another division at Nissho Iwai where I worked. She called him to make the introduction and he invited me out for tea during break time.

The next day, my Nissho Iwai mentor asked me how I knew that gentleman. I told him of the connection. He did not say more. But I found out later that my new friend had been gently reprimanded, told, that it was not appropriate to go out with me alone. I was considered unaware; he was considered in the know. They saved me from any potential whispers or gossip, and he saved face because it all happened behind the scenes.

Wow. Japan is a well-oiled wheel of appropriateness and communication where everything gets done in the proper way and no one is embarrassed.

The Japanese company is like a big family. Women colleagues are treated professionally and yet protected like sisters. Sometimes the salaries of women are less than men, even today, so when the group goes out after work, the women will only pay in direct proportion to their smaller salary.

Being a Woman Can Be an Advantage

In the Gulf countries, such as the United Arab Emirates (which includes Abu Dhabi and Dubai), Saudi Arabia, Oman, Qatar, Iraq, Kuwait, and Bahrain, women are taken care of more, and you can use this to your advantage if you need help. In the Mediterranean Arab countries, such as Lebanon and Jordan, there is a more general equality between men and women.

Capable Western women might have an easier time being accepted into business than capable local women.

Be sure, however, to interact conservatively, because even if a Western woman is married, any inappropriateness will most likely trigger a sexual advance.

Foreign businesswomen should dress like the locals. You can wear the traditional baggy pants so you cannot see the shape of your figure. In some places, you may need to cover more.

Personal questions are not considered inappropriate. Marriage and children are common questions, because lineage is important to these cultures. They are basically asking "Who is your family?"

Points to Remember: Women in Cross-Cultural Business

- Understand when personal questions are appropriate and when they are not.

- Dress appropriately for the culture where you are.

- Be informed of social customs for men and women in business.

- Meet other local professional woman to ask them for advice.

Women around the world are dedicated educators. Uzbek teachers in Isfana, Kyrgyzstan.

In a Kyrgyz carpet-making collective, several women make the carpets together for sale. I tried a few stitches and it was not easy.

Artisans share techniques and form collectives and NGOs to create collaborative businesses.

LESSON 17:

Silence Is Golden

Ma, The Pregnant Pause

Americans and Westerners are often confused about the role of silence in communication and business meetings.

The Japanese language is indirect, polite, and leaves room for interpretation.

Silence can be golden. Asians are comfortable with silence. *Ma* means "space" or "pause" in Japanese. I call it the pregnant pause.

In Japan, a common error is to talk over someone or interrupt them. You not only need to wait until someone is finished, but you also need to give a long pause to show you have absorbed the information into your gut before commenting. Premature comments and talking are considered immature. The more mature and, therefore, wise a person is, the more he or she waits patiently to comment.

On the other hand, in Central and South America, and Latin countries in Europe, talking for long periods of time or two or three people interrupting or overlapping comments while someone is still speaking is the norm—it is not considered rude.

In Japan, there is also the invisible dynamic of connecting to the gut, to the *hara*, and to feel the deeper intuitive energy

157

within yourself as well as between yourself and another. These silent spaces, the pregnant pauses, may seem a waste of time to Westerners, but they are very deep cues and ways to gather nonverbal information.

Breathe deeply, be aware, take your time to respond.

And know that the Japanese businesspeople in a meeting who seem to be asleep are most likely closing their eyes and feeling the room and people from a gut level, taking it all in without rushing.

The Concept of *Haragei*—The Art of Business Negotiation in Japan

It is important to be in touch with your intuition and gut instincts in Japan. It is called *haragei,* or the Art of Hara, and is a way of being beyond the mind, drawing power from your gut. *Hara* means "belly," your "honorable middle," the center of your physical body. It is what grounds you.

It is your source, the navel center, where all your vital organs are. It is where the most important connection is. The art of hara is about drawing deep power from your center.

Haragei relates to charisma and strength of personality. In the Japanese language, to have a big *hara* means to be generous. I see this as being open, vulnerable, and authentic, like the Buddha. To have a black *hara* is to be corrupt, evil. To have no *hara* means not yet developed, green behind the ears, immature, and is considered an insult. "He/she has no *hara*" can especially be used when someone is not able to keep their emotions in check in business meetings. But to have *hara* means one can stomach both friends and enemies with equanimity.

Haragei is about expressing intentions in more ways than just direct speech. This includes vagueness, nonverbal cues such as facial expressions, eye contact or no eye contact, and long silences. Timing is important.

I witnessed one of the most profound displays of silence and *haragei* in 1992. I arranged for my yoga guru, Yogi Amrit Desai, from the U.S., to do a seminar tour in Japan. I took him one morning at 5 a.m. to meet my former martial arts master, Doshu Kisshomaru Ueshiba, the elderly son of the founder of Aikido. I had expected to translate some deep discussion between them about the spirituality of aikido and yoga. After greeting each other they drank green tea. They sat. They breathed into their *hara* centers. They make eye contact. They lowered their eyes. They sat in silence. About thirty minutes later, I thanked the Aikido Master with a full kneeling bow. After we left, I mentioned to my guru that I thought they would have something to talk about. He replied, "We were communicating. We did not need to say anything."

Points to Remember About Silence in Japan

- Silence is important to show you are absorbing information.

- *Haragei* is about listening to your intuition and gut instincts.

- It is also about communicating nonverbally.

LESSON 18

Harmony, Persuasion, and Confrontation

Some cultures are careful to keep their actions and communications indirect to maintain a team spirit and harmonious relationships. Other cultures are more direct and are not afraid to express disagreement.

To people who communicate more directly, the indirect approach can seem evasive and untrustworthy. To people who communicate more indirectly, the direct approach can seem impolite and confrontational.

Persuasion or argumentation styles vary in different cultures. There are three general ways you can use to influence other people. Use a logical approach, a sentimental or emotional approach, or a historical approach influencing them with tradition.

"Yes" Can Mean "No"

Depending upon the circumstances, some people will answer "yes" when they really mean "no" or "maybe" in order to avoid what can be perceived as confrontational.

Japanese leaders know the Art of *Hara* (see Lesson 17). In Japanese business negotiations, *haragei* can be used when "yes" means "no."

Here is an example. When former President Richard Nixon asked former Prime Minister Eisaku Sato to limit exports in 1970, Sato replied "I will do my best." Nixon took this as a "yes." Sato was saying "no." To say "no" directly would have been contrary to *haragei*.

A misunderstanding like the one between Nixon and Sato, caused by cross-cultural differences, can make or break a relationship in a global world.

TIP: Beware of How You Ask Questions to Get a Clearer Yes or No

Person A: "You don't want to go out to eat, right?"

Person B: "Yes." (She means "I want to go.")

Person C: "Yes." (She means: "I don't want to go. Your full statement is correct.")

Person D: "No." (She means "I don't want to go.")

Person E: "No." (She means "Your statement is not correct. I do want to go.")

To avoid confusion, Person A could have simply asked, "Do you want to go out to eat?"

Watch What You Ask For

Failure is perceived is various ways. Americans tend to set high goals, and if they are not reached, they analyze the points for improvement and then just try again and again.

Sometimes "No" can mean "Yes."

You need to be aware of how you ask something of someone, the expectations you set, and how they are perceived and could be misunderstood.

In Japan, I was the lead go-between for a joint venture between the local government of a town in Japan and a U.S. health and wellness facility. The Japanese wanted to expand their resort activities since they were primarily a skiing location and did not have summer business.

To preface these meetings, I set up a series of health and wellness lectures and seminars for the U.S. CEO in various Japanese locations.

When I discussed this with my long-term friends in Japan, they kept asking me, "How many people to you need to attend?" I did not understand how to answer, so I took my goal of what might be a good number in the U.S. and said 500.

I was surprised when my friends, who had done so much for me and me for them, said, "Sorry, we cannot help you." I did not understand that what they were saying was, "We cannot guarantee that number so we cannot help you at all because to try to get 500 and to fall short, would mean we had failed." Then they would lose face.

They could not try for 500 and then have 350 and say, "We did our best."

I worked really hard and had some degree of success. In the end my Japanese friends asked how many showed up, and I said there had been enough, but not 500.

They said "If we had known you would be okay with less than 500, we could have each brought ten friends. You could have had even more with us there."

Lesson learned. Do not be specific about expectations until you know what is possible.

In the U.S., a friend trying their best is enough. But in Japan, it is not. They have to meet your expectations.

Harmony with History

Just because you do not talk about something does not mean it is forgotten. In many cultures, history is considered over, and harmony is strived for in the present and future.

I was only twenty-four when I traveled Marco Polo's Silk Route from Spain to Nepal to finally reach Japan, where I lived in total immersion for many years. I had never met any Japanese people before, and what most stuck out in my mind about Japan was World War II. I thought the Japanese would not like me because I was an American. My landlady's husband was the first Japanese veteran I met. He showed me his traditional army gear and then told me, "We are friends now." As a young adult, this really impacted me. It seemed a Zen-like comment that we experienced the past but we can live in the present. It was a welcome to my new life in Japan.

Points to Remember about Harmony, Persuasion, and Confrontation

- In some cultures it is acceptable to express disagreement, while in others it is avoided to maintain harmony.

- Sometimes, the aversion towards confrontation is so strong, people will say "yes" when they mean "no."

- Failure is perceived differently across cultures.

LESSON 19

Business Meetings, Negotiating, and Decision-Making as an American Manager Overseas

Business meetings, negotiating, and decision-making encompass distinct differences in different cultures. To make it even more complicated, you also have to consider distinct corporate cultures, company policies, and the nature of each individual involved.

Advanced preparation and research, cultural awareness, and asking questions ahead of time can definitely help. But as with life itself, interacting with people involves an element of the unexpected. Therefore, your own confidence, openness, personal emotional control, and respect for others are important.

Working in Other Cultures

Many U.S. multinational corporations send American managers to subsidiaries overseas. When the rest of the staff are all locals, the American style of management will need to change to accommodate the cultural norms of that local group.

It goes both ways, though. American-style management and communication exposure will help those in the foreign subsidiary to expand their cross-cultural awareness.

When there is no time to quietly observe and follow the lead of others before assuming a role of authority in a different culture, you can help to speed up your own cultural awareness by asking a knowledgeable, trustworthy and appropriately positioned local about their communication practices. A professionally trained cross-cultural coach can help as well.

To begin your process of getting ready for cross-cultural communication, copy and fill in the preparation guide below. Yes/No questions (and a few open-ended ones for reflection) will heighten your awareness of your own assumptions and preferences. Use the extra space provided to expand upon your answers.

Preparation Guide

Cross-Cultural Business Relations and Communications

- Is it acceptable to discuss business right away?
  ☐ Yes   ☐ No

- Do you need to develop a relationship with someone before doing business with them?
  ☐ Yes   ☐ No

- Do you need a formal introduction to initiate contact?
  ☐ Yes   ☐ No

- Is helping a friend more important than doing what is right or correct?

  ☐ Yes   ☐ No

  _____

  _____

- Do you value your relationships, even if they do not have a direct business advantage?

  ☐ Yes   ☐ No

  _____

  _____

For Further Reflection

- Do you say what you think, or do you say what you think others want to hear?

  _____

  _____

  _____

- Do you use "I" statements or say "we" instead?

  _____

  _____

  _____

- Are relationships formed among all levels of employees? Or are coworker relationships quite distinct from relationships with superiors and bosses?

  _____

  _____

  _____

- Are communications brief and vague, or are they lengthy and detailed to avoid all potential problems?

_____

_____

_____

Negotiating

- Does an individual person have the power to make decisions in a business deal?

  ☐ Yes   ☐ No

_____

_____

- Do you consider how your actions will affect the team?

  ☐ Yes   ☐ No

_____

_____

- Are you consensus-oriented?

  ☐ Yes   ☐ No

_____

_____

- Is your approach for a win-win outcome in which each party gets what they want?

  ☐ Yes   ☐ No

_____

_____

- Are there strict deadlines?

  ☐ Yes   ☐ No

_____

_____

- Do you focus on objectives for the future success and growth?

  ☐ Yes   ☐ No

  _____

  _____

- Are the outcomes of previous negotiations important?

  ☐ Yes   ☐ No

  _____

  _____

- Are emotional displays acceptable in business meetings?

  ☐ Yes   ☐ No

  _____

  _____

- Is compromise the assumed outcome?

  ☐ Yes   ☐ No

  _____

  _____

- Are you direct or indirect in your negotiating style?

  ☐ Yes   ☐ No

  _____

  _____

For Further Reflection

- Do you begin discussing negotiations right away? Or is the prenegotiation trust-building process crucial?

  _____

  _____

- Are negotiations summarized in detailed documents? Or is a handshake enough?

  _____

  _____

- Is a signed contract final? Or, is it only the beginning of more renegotiation?

  _____

  _____

- Do you consider only the final result of a particular negotiation, or do you focus on the bigger picture (relationships, long-term business potential, timelines, etc.)?

  _____

  _____

- Who is empowered to make decisions? (i.e., what is their status, gender, age, and so on?)

  _____

  _____

- Do several people get involved in negotiations, regardless of rank? Or do the senior negotiators have the final say?

  _____

  _____

Making Decisions

- Are you quick to offer decisions?
  ☐ Yes   ☐ No

  _____

  _____

- Do you avoid giving answers on the spot?

  ☐ Yes   ☐ No

  _____

  _____

- Do you consult everyone involved and therefore move more slowly?

  ☐ Yes   ☐ No

  _____

  _____

- Do you need to go through a chain of command to come back with a decision?

  ☐ Yes   ☐ No

  _____

  _____

- Are decisions based on logic and need to be justified?

  ☐ Yes   ☐ No

  _____

  _____

- Is there a consideration for human differences?

  ☐ Yes   ☐ No

  _____

  _____

- Do you need to ask questions to clarify because of subtleties when meaning is implied but not expressed?

  ☐ Yes   ☐ No

  _____

  _____

- Is a decision based on how an individual can advance his or her own position?

  ☐ Yes   ☐ No

  _____

  _____

For Further Reflection

- Is the speed of a decision valued? Or are they carefully thought out, causing delays?

  _____

  _____

- Are new ideas valued, or are they challenged?

  _____

  _____

- Are decisions made with minimal information, or do you hold off until you know every little detail?

  _____

  _____

- Is open criticism valued as truthfulness? Or do you avoid disagreement?

  _____

  _____

Making Effective Presentations

- Do you focus on facts and figures and the end result?

  ☐ Yes   ☐ No

  _____

  _____

- Or are your presentations lengthy, with details of past business dealings?

  ☐ Yes ☐ No

_____

_____

For Further Reflection

- Do your presentations rely mostly on hard data, or do you use anecdotes and real life scenarios?

_____

_____

- Do you use an interactive coaching style eliciting input and dialogue from those you are presenting to?

_____

_____

- Do you include time for Q & A and discussions?

_____

_____

- Are you comfortable being interrupted during your presentation with questions?

_____

_____

- Are you selling your ideas during a presentation, or do you let the facts speak for themselves?

_____

_____

Running Effective Meetings

- Is punctuality important?

  ☐ Yes   ☐ No

  _____

  _____

- Are personal obligations an acceptable excuse for being late, not being prepared, or missing a deadline?

  ☐ Yes   ☐ No

  _____

  _____

- Is one agenda item discussed at a time?

  ☐ Yes   ☐ No

  _____

  _____

- Do you need to be 100% sure ideas will be accepted before suggesting them?

  ☐ Yes   ☐ No

  _____

  _____

For Further Reflection

- Do you like a back-and-forth communication style and open-ended dialogue of individual ideas, or is your goal to come to a group consensus?

  _____

  _____

Last question: Did you expect the Preparation Guide to include a scoring system or a tally so you could add up and categorize your responses, put them into a formula, and then get a specific action plan for how to approach working in your new setting?

Remember: You are working with people, not statistics. Each person and situation is unique. I include these questions to help you think and become more aware of what to notice and respond to in the moment.

After you've gathered your own answers, you can also use the Preparation Guide as a framework to speak with a few colleagues in your new culture to gain insights into their preferences and practices.

LESSON 20

Cross-Cultural Approaches to Team-Building, Project Management, and Feedback

To help you become aware of your own experience and business culture, you need to identify and consider your own assumptions and social culture and how they may differ from your business partners and colleagues elsewhere in the world.

As you answer the following questions, you will be on the way to recognizing cross-cultural differences more easily. Take note of what your answers to these questions are; observe with your actual experiences and you will find patterns that will help you in the future as well.

You will also find the same questions useful when you are getting to know business partners from another culture.

Preparation Guide

Team Building

- Do you like to show your talent and acknowledge the individual skills of others?

  ☐ Yes   ☐ No

_____

_____

- When something goes wrong, do you need to know whose mishap it was?

  ☐ Yes   ☐ No

  _____

  _____

- Do all team members treat each other as equals?

  ☐ Yes   ☐ No

  _____

  _____

- Is everyone expected to contribute to problem-solving and brainstorming sessions?

  ☐ Yes   ☐ No

  _____

  _____

- Does the team want a decision to seem like a group effort rather than a specific person's idea?

  ☐ Yes   ☐ No

  _____

  _____

- Does the team wait to be told what to do by their superiors?

  ☐ Yes   ☐ No

  _____

  _____

- Are expertise and experience valued highly?

  ☐ Yes   ☐ No

  _____

  _____

- Are forward-thinkers with new ideas the stars of the team?
  ☐ Yes   ☐ No

_____

_____

- Do you adopt new ideas, processes and business practices easily?
  ☐ Yes   ☐ No

_____

_____

- Do you feel uncomfortable when there's quick change?
  ☐ Yes   ☐ No

_____

_____

- Do you like to consider all unknown possibilities before making a decision?
  ☐ Yes   ☐ No

_____

_____

- Do you appreciate direct, honest information from the leader?
  ☐ Yes   ☐ No

_____

_____

- Can conflicts be discussed openly?
  ☐ Yes   ☐ No

_____

_____

- Do you take confrontations personally?
  ☐ Yes   ☐ No

  _____

  _____

- Is the team leader the one with the best leadership skills, regardless of experience and length of time with the company?
  ☐ Yes   ☐ No

  _____

  _____

- Is work-life balance important?
  ☐ Yes   ☐ No

  _____

  _____

- Are you achievement-oriented? Do you work overtime, weekends, and holidays?
  ☐ Yes   ☐ No

  _____

  _____

For Further Reflection

- Is everyone on the team subject to the same rules and processes? Or is it fairer to treat people differently based on their individual situations?

  _____

  _____

- Is it best to focus on the task assigned to the team and define the individual roles required? Or is it best to focus on the relationships among people within the team?

  _____

  _____

- Do you only express the results you expect from the team before setting them on task to achieve them? Or do you set clear guidelines about the process you want them to follow?

  _____

  _____

- Are you more comfortable with short- or long-term relationships?

  _____

  _____

Project Management

- Do you work on projects independently?
  ☐ Yes   ☐ No

  _____

  _____

- Do you tend to feel micromanaged and left without space to prove yourself?
  ☐ Yes   ☐ No

  _____

  _____

For Further Reflection

- Do you like to exchange ideas or check in with others while working on a project?

_____

_____

- Do you expect timeliness and take deadlines literally, or do you give individuals leeway to go at their own pace?

_____

_____

- Is a personal matter a valid excuse for not finishing a project on time?

_____

_____

- How much do you oversee a project? E.g., do you ask for periodic updates?

_____

_____

Rewards, Recognition, Criticism, and Feedback

- How do you prefer to give feedback? Privately or in front of the group? Does it depend on whether it's praise or criticism?

_____

_____

- Do you reward someone for an outstanding job or good performance? What?

_____

_____

- Do you give praise to the whole team or single out individuals?

_____

_____

- Do you give criticism by highlighting positive points first, or do you just dive into the criticism and points that need improvement?

_____

_____

Establishing Credibility, Mentoring, and Status

- Are authority and credibility based on demonstrated competency?
  ☐ Yes   ☐ No

_____

_____

- Do you look to a person's experience, age, and status as the basis of authority?
  ☐ Yes   ☐ No

_____

_____

- Do you have a mentor?
  ☐ Yes   ☐ No

_____

_____

- Do you mentor others?

  ☐ Yes   ☐ No

Information Exchange, Gathering, and Sharing

- Do you keep information private?

  ☐ Yes   ☐ No

- Are you suspicious of people who keep information private?

  ☐ Yes   ☐ No

- Do you share openly with the group?

  ☐ Yes   ☐ No

- How do you feel about sharing privileged information within the team?

  ☐ Yes   ☐ No

Style of Leadership

- Do you take charge?

  ☐ Yes   ☐ No

  _____

  _____

- Do you empower your staff to make their own decisions?

  ☐ Yes   ☐ No

  _____

  _____

- Are you collaborative?

  ☐ Yes   ☐ No

  _____

  _____

- Do you value interdependence?

  ☐ Yes   ☐ No

  _____

  _____

Virtual Communications, Emails, Faxes

- Do you communicate individual-to-individual, rarely copying others on written communications?

  ☐ Yes   ☐ No

  _____

  _____

- Do you copy the entire team on all communications?

  ☐ Yes   ☐ No

  _____

  _____

- Do you expect a prompt reply?

  ☐ Yes   ☐ No

  _____

  _____

- Do you give ample information ahead of time and wait patiently for a response?

  ☐ Yes   ☐ No

  _____

  _____

- Do you reply to an email even if you do not have the answer?

  ☐ Yes   ☐ No

  _____

  _____

- Are your emails lengthy or short?

  ☐ Yes   ☐ No

  _____

  _____

Reflect upon your answers. Notice new perspectives on how you interact with your team, manage projects, and give and receive feedback. Consider what is particular to you as an individual, what the norm is in your company or profession, and what you observe in others from a different culture.

You can also use the Preparation Guide as a framework for discussions with your counterparts to lay the groundwork for better communication.

Kyrgyz and Uzbek teachers collaborate, share, and create new techniques for English classes in Harriet's day-long coaching workshop.

SECTION III

Landing *On Your Feet* in a Different Country

Greetings, Forms of Address, Business Cards

First impressions count. When you meet someone, it is important to know what is culturally acceptable and not acceptable in that business environment. Do you kiss, bow, or shake hands? Do you need a calling card? Do you call people by title, first, or last name?

Kiss, Hug, or Shake Hands

- In the United States and many Western countries we shake hands. But who goes first? And is it always necessary? In first-time business encounters, handshakes may not always be expected, but it is proper etiquette. Universally, a woman has the option to extend her hand first.

- The Ukrainians consider it bad luck to shake hands over the threshold of a doorway.

- Once you know the person and upon subsequent meetings or in daily interactions, a handshake is no longer necessary.

- In Mexico, Central America, South America, and European Latin countries of Spain, Portugal, France, and Italy, there is a lot of hugging and kissing. Men hug men, and so do women hug women. Women often use the "air kiss" with men. Depending on the country, it may be two or three kisses. A pat on the back, a touch on the arm, or a hug is common in the workplace.

- In Chile, men will usually shake hands in business. Women are greeted with one kiss on the right cheek.

To Bow or Not to Bow

In many cultures, bowing is a prevalent custom. It can be a greeting upon arrival and departure, or an acknowledgement of someone else's presence. It shows respect and submission or deference to someone of a higher status. It is a gesture of gratitude. It can also be used as an apology. There is a complex etiquette with many nuances depending on who is bowing, who is being bowed to, the circumstances for the bow, and what message is being conveyed.

- In Western countries, we do not bow in business settings. But it is used all the time in many parts of Asia and East Asia, such as Japan, Korea, Taiwan, China and Vietnam. However, in Taiwan, China, and Vietnam, a slight bow with a handshake is more popular than a full bow.

- When one person is Asian and another is a Westerner, sometimes a handshake and bow are combined, or one can follow the other.

- Folded hands in a prayer gesture along with a bow is common in South and Southeast Asia in Sri Lanka, Nepal, India, Bhutan, Thailand, Cambodia, Laos, Myanmar, and Indonesia.

- You can perhaps relate to the meaning of the bow from our history of kneeling and curtsies. Stage performers bow at curtain call, thanking their supporters and receiving applause with humility.

- A nod of the head can be regarded as a minimal form of bow. For example, in England, Australia and other Commonwealth countries, lawyers perform a cursory bow of the head when the judge enters or leaves a courtroom.

- The deeper and longer the bow, the more formal it is.

- The Japanese kneel with the head to the ground in martial arts and the tea ceremony. In the Buddhist temples in Tibet, I watched the elderly villagers fully prostrate themselves and get up again 108 times daily as they circumambulated the temple with pads on their knees for protection and rollers on their hands to slide more easily.

- Not only is the depth of the bow important, but also how long you hold it. Two or three seconds is enough in a business setting. If you hold longer, the other person will need to bow again to be polite, which leads to a series of bows between the parties each one progressively lighter until you are both standing again. It is like getting the last word in, except the exchange is not for your ego to win, but for your ego to be humbled. A bow is a lowering of the ego, a sign of humility and respect.

- A manager or supervisor only nods the head slightly or not at all when addressing a subordinate while the subordinate bows.

Degrees of bowing in Japan

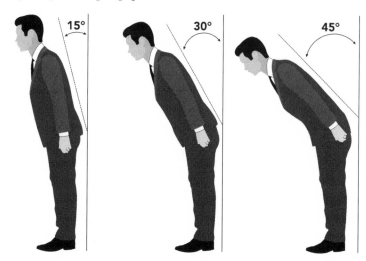

| Greeting bow (*eshaku*) for bowing to same status | Respectful bow (*keirei*) for bowing to higher status | Deep respectful bow (*saikeirei*) for when apologizing or asking favors |

The good news is that no one expects a Westerner to know the nuances of the custom of bowing. So ask ahead of time about the bowing customs of where you are doing business, observe what others do, and follow them. They will be pleased you tried and not fault you if you do not do it perfectly.

Other Forms of Greeting

Kyrgyz men in traditional hats using both hands for a handshake.

In Kyrgyzstan, I observed the men greet each other by putting the right hand over their own heart as a greeting of respect. Young and old, women and men will use this greeting when serving tea. Men will also hold both hands at once instead of a one-handed shake. However, in business settings in the capital Bishkek, the Western handshake is used between men.

Do not extend your hand to an Arab Muslim woman or touch her. I advise Western businesswomen not to shake hands with Arab Muslims to keep with local custom. If the man extends his hand first, you may choose.

Forms of Address

Americans, both men and women, quickly move to a first-name basis in business.

It is not uncommon for some cultures to use only the title of a person to address them—for example, Doktor in

German for someone with a PhD, or Professor in English, or Sensei in Japanese for a master of any subject or person of much higher position.

I have been called Mrs. Harriet in many countries for added respect as a mentor, and because of my age.

In China, titles in a hierarchy are important. However, a newer trend is title inflation. A business card may read "Director" in both English and Chinese, but that person could be just the equivalent of a manager.

What if you are unsure of how to address someone? Observe others. Listen for titles, full names, and nicknames. Observe who is using them and what status they have.

Feel free to ask them to repeat their name again more slowly. This shows you really want to know it, and ensures you'll remember it and pronounce it better in the future.

If you don't know what to call a person of higher status, asking them directly might not get you an answer. If you are unsure, ask someone else, "What should I call your company Director?"

In Spain, as a young twenty-one-year-old English tutor for a wealthy family, I asked the Señora of the house if I should use the informal *tu* or the formal *usted* form of address for "you." I was confused. I was invited to lunch with the family every day, and I was not one of the servants. She replied that it depended upon how I felt. Considering my younger age, and because I wanted to show her respect as my employer and a woman of status, I continued to address her as *usted*.

Another hint was that she did not ask me to call her any differently. It is rare for a person of status to ask you to address them more formally, but if they want you to use a more familiar form of address, they will tell you.

Take the example of all those 800 number customer service calls. "Hello. My name is Marilyn. How can I help you, Mrs. Russell?" I then reply, "Please call me Harriet." And the conversation continues. When Japanese and Chinese deal with Westerners and speak English, they will use their first name to step into your culture. They may shorten their name to make it easier for you to pronounce. For example, Kenichi or Kentaro can become Ken.

You are probably not the only person wondering about titles. Colleagues and acquaintances may wonder what to call you. They may not be able to pronounce your name.

Help them out. "Please call me…" And say your name slowly and clearly.

Foreigners speaking English often talk very slowly only to speed up when saying their name. Don't make the same mistake.

In Japan and China, first and last names are reversed. Always stay on a last name basis. In Japan, just attach the honorific -san to the end of the last name to add the meaning Mr., Mrs., or Miss. If you are personal close friends and on a first name basis, then attach -san to the first name.

The Holy Business Card

The Japanese *meishi* business card is almost holy.

How it is written, what your title is, to whom you give it, and how you present it all have their rules and regulations in business etiquette.

When I worked in New York City, I joined the Japan Society, which offered access to international business and policy leaders, in-depth networking opportunities, and cultural programs. There I met a senior executive of Mitsui & Co. After a conversation about my upcoming internship in Nissho Iwai Corporation, Tokyo, the Mitsui executive gave me his business card. The unique point is that on the blank back of the card, he wrote the name of another senior executive in Nissho Iwai. They had been friends at the same university and at one time worked together.

This was a special introduction. Little did I realize that this card was a golden gift.

I kept the card for a couple weeks when I first arrived in Japan. When I gave it to my mentor, he was amazed. "How did you get this? How do you know him?" And then he said, "Why did you wait? This is a very busy man and it will be difficult to meet him in this short time of several months." I did not even know the power of that signed card.

It turned out I was the catalyst for the Mitsui executive to meet with his counterpart executive in Nissho Iwai on his return to Japan. A chauffeur took us in a limo to a private luncheon club, which did not even have a sign on the door. Two top near-retirement executives and young me.

I sat the entire time without saying a word and hardly being spoken to. I was the card deliverer. I was the holder of a business card which by the mere handwritten name on the back became an invitation. My role was to just observe these high-powered men as they reconnected.

Patience. They had waited thirty years to connect. But the connection in Japan is long-term, forever.

HARRIET L. RUSSELL, M.S.
Lecturer, Japanese Language
Cross Cultural Communications
Dept. of Foreign Languages and Literatures

275 Eastland Rd.
Berea, OH 44017, U.S.A.

Tel: (216) 826-2249
Fax:(216) 826-3021

科学修士
ハリエット・ラッセル
講師、日本語
異文化間コミュニケーション
外国語・外国文学学部

ボールドウィン
ワラス大学

米国オハイオ州ベレア市
イーストランド・ロード275番
〒 44017

Tel: (216) 826-2249
Fax: (216) 826-3021

Bhumi's
Be Healthy Under My Instruction

Харриет Русселль
Директор

+1-440-236-6366
Harriet@BhumiInternational.com
www.BhumiInternational.com

- Межкультурные связи
- Индивидуальный бытовой коучинг
- Программы стрессменеджмента на рабочем месте
- Сертификационные обучения тренеров йоги
- Лекции

www.BhumiInternational.com

One of my old Japanese business cards and my old Russian business cards. (Note: The data on these business cards is no longer current.)

199

Business Card Rules in Japan

- Never put it in your back pocket.

- Never write notes on it.

- Take it with both hands and bow. The importance of exchanging cards is worthy of a ritual.

- In a meeting, line up the cards in the order of seating and hierarchy. Ponder each one. Take them in.

- A business card without a title is worthless. How can the Japanese know how to address you if they do not know your status and position?

In the U.S., we often write a note on our business card with an extra piece of contact information or on theirs as a reminder of how to follow up. And there is no ritual of card exchange.

Exchanging business cards at the Rotary Club in Minsk, Belarus.

Giving, Receiving, Declining Gifts

To Gift or Not To Gift

Gift-giving is a worldwide custom. A gift in its purest intention is given without an explicit agreement for immediate or future rewards. It is not a form of barter or payment.

However, in developing relationships, gifts show a desire to connect, to open the door, to appreciate the opportunity to build a future, and to share a part of one's culture.

It is important to realize, however, that the specifics of gift-giving are not the same in all cultures. All good intentions aside, one could unknowingly convey a wrong message, and what may be appropriate in one country could be entirely a faux pas in another.

In business, gift-giving can be an even more tricky experience. Some considerations are:

- Where do we draw the line between business and personal gifts?
- Even though a gift may be paid for from a personal account and not as a business expense, is it appropriate to give gifts?
- If so, what kind?
- Is there a price limit?
- When do we give the gift?

- Is the gift to initiate a connection or to celebrate a successful negotiation?

- To whom should we give the gift?

- Should we give it in front of others or privately?

In some countries, you do not open the gift in front of the giver. It would seem you are being greedy. In other countries, it is an insult not to open it immediately.

For example, in Russia children's gifts are opened in private, but adult gifts are opened in front of others.

In China, Ukraine, and Morocco, gifts are not opened in front of the giver, but in Italy, Greece, Spain, Germany, Norway, or Ireland, gifts are opened immediately when received.

A client of mine working at NASA was given a small gift of minimal value by a Japanese visitor. He wondered why. He responded with doubt and hesitation because it was not something he commonly experienced. Was it just a nice gesture? Or would NASA consider it a bribe?

Japan: The Epitome of Gift-Giving

Gift-giving holds various degrees of importance in different parts of the world. It is of lowest importance in Australia, Canada, United States, and European countries In Latin American countries and the Middle East, and some Pacific Rim Asian countries like Korea, Taiwan, China, Malaysia, or Thailand, it is of medium importance.

Japan outshines them all. Here it is of utmost importance. The country is the epitome of a gift-giving culture, more so in terms of frequency and not necessarily cost, but gifts are always wrapped exquisitely.

I was working at Nissho Iwai Corporation, a trading company in Japan. The Division Head called his executive secretary and me into his office. We were served tea first, and he then gave the secretary a gift box with a piece of jewelry inside. After she accepted the gift with a bow, he handed me a substantially more expensive silver, gold, and Akoya pearl brooch, since my status was higher as the only international trainee and honorable guest. Jewelry is usually not an acceptable business gift, especially when given from a man to a woman; however, this brooch was made by one of the company's subsidiaries. He wanted to give me a remembrance gift from the company. At the same time, it was important for him to abide by proper protocol and etiquette. He therefore needed to have his secretary present to also receive a similar gift. As it was a December day, he cushioned the gesture even more by wishing me a Merry Christmas. If he had not given me the jewelry in the way he did, the nature and cost of the gift would have carried a different message.

Gift-giving is so important in Japan there's a whole week dedicated to it. In the first week of the New Year, the Japanese give gifts to clients, professors and teachers as an appreciation for their business or mentorship.

Giving Gifts Across the World

In **Costa Rica**, for business negotiations gift-giving is standard and customary. It could be offensive to give fruit or coffee, since Costa Rica is renowned for these. Always wrap your gift in nice paper, but not black or purple which are colors of the Holy Week. Thank-you notes are important and should not be overlooked. In business, to avoid misunderstanding, men should use caution when giving a female colleague a gift by saying it is from his secretary or wife.

Even in the **U.S.**, we have male-female protocols. When I was a Boston University student going to Spain, my boss at work gave me $100. His wife signed the card and check, and so I accepted it. When I returned I brought a $15 souvenir for them both. This covered any potential inappropriate insinuations.

In general, in **Latin America** gift-giving is not as ritualistic as in Asia or the Middle East, but it does play an important role. It reinforces business relations as personal relations as it shows thoughtfulness and generosity. When gifts are carefully chosen, it demonstrates awareness and respect. Avoid leather gifts because most of the world's finest leathers come from South America.

Brazilians do value hospitality, but they do not give gifts in the business sector. They are not expected, and they can be considered a bribe. Do not give a gift, even on the first meeting. If you want to give a gift, save it for a social occasion. A scarf for a helpful female secretary is good, but if the giver is a man, say "This is from my wife." Good gifts in general are stylish, name-brand pens and accessories, small electronic items, good quality whisky, coffee-table books, and U.S. sports team and university apparel. Something expensive will cause embarrassment, and avoid fine keychains, wallets, and jewelry, as these are too personal. Also do not give anything with the number thirteen which is bad luck: purple or black items; flowers, which are a reminder of mourning; and handkerchiefs, which are associated with tears and funerals.

In many countries, such as Switzerland, Germany, **Netherlands**, **Brazil**, **Egypt**, and the **U.S.**, sharp objects such as knives and scissors represent bad luck and imply severing the relationship. Once, my mother wanted to give me a set of high quality knives. But she asked me to buy them for $1. That way they were no longer a gift, but a purchase, so as not to sever our relationship.

In **Australia**, **Canada**, the **U.S.**, and **European** countries, business gifts are rarely expected. They are seen as a nice gesture but small gifts are usually sufficient. Avoid gifts that will be perceived as bribes. When visiting the home of a business colleague, it is normally appropriate to bring a gift for the hostess, like flowers or wine. But avoid giving German wine when in Germany—stick to French or Italian. And in France, avoid giving wine altogether, as the hostess prefers to choose the vintage for the evening.

In **England**, business gift-giving is not part of the business culture. If you give a gift to your British business counterparts, they might be embarrassed. If you still want to give a gift, save it until the conclusion of a deal. It should be small and tasteful, a desk accessory or paperweight or book about your country. Although unlikely, if you receive a gift and do not have one to give back, inviting someone out to a meal can be seen as a gift.

Irish business culture does not exchange corporate gifts, but small gifts are appropriate for business social events, like a bottle of wine or gift from your home country. Many Irish businesspeople are golfers with business done on the golf course, so golf gifts are popular, and your club logo or hometown identity on them is fine. A one-time polite refusal is appropriate when the gift is first offered.

In **Spain**, a high-context culture (see Lesson 10), initial business meetings are simply to get to know you before doing business. Exchange gifts only when successful business negotiations are concluded. Business gifts should be of good quality, but not too expensive or extravagant, or they may be perceived as bribes.

Austrians are more interested in the extent of your education and the length of time your company has been in business. They will do business with you without a personal relationship and gift-giving is not a business norm.

Do not give a gift in the **Netherlands** unless you already know the recipient. The Dutch reserve gifts for close personal relationships. The same goes in **Ukraine**, where the act of gift-giving is considered a symbol of friendship. If invited into a Dutch or Ukrainian home, you can bring a bouquet of flowers or send one the following day as a thank-you.

In **Germany**, a low-context culture (see Lesson 10), a small gift is polite when you make contacts for the first time, but after that gifts are not usual, and certainly not before a successful deal is made. However, small gifts to office staff who assisted you during your visit are not expected but will be appreciated. Larger, more substantial gifts should be given more officially in public, not in private. As for being invited into a German home, bring chocolates, fresh flowers, or yellow roses. (Avoid carnations, which symbolize mourning; lilies and chrysanthemums, which are for funerals; and red roses, which represent romance.) Talking of red roses, in **Portugal**, avoid red flowers all together as red is the symbol of the revolution and considered offensive.

At a senior management level, business gifts are given in **Italy**. They should be of good quality, but not overly expensive. Small gifts are fine for co-workers and staff, but company logo gifts are in bad taste. Food and liquor are good gifts, but remember Italians are wine connoisseurs.

Inquiring about your Italian colleagues' family and personal interests before meeting them will help to forge your relationship. Choose an appropriate and personalized gift if you can. If there are children in the family, bring small gifts for them too. Gifts should be wrapped, but not in black, the color of mourning, or purple, which symbolizes bad luck and death. When you are invited to a social event, you can bring wine, chocolates, pastries, or flowers as a thank you. A homemade food gift is considered a labor of love. You can also give an extra gift to the wife for her meal preparation.

If you want to give your Italian hostess flowers, have them delivered earlier in the day. Avoid red, which indicates secrecy; yellow, which symbolizes jealously; and chrysanthemums, which are for funerals. Do not give seventeen of anything, as it is an unlucky number. Also avoid giving brooches, handkerchiefs, or knives, because these are associated with sadness. And remember to never mention the price of a gift.

Business gift-giving in **Sweden** is unusual, even on holidays. Holiday cards are appropriate to thank people for their business in that year. However, a business gift is appropriate if you close a business deal. Make it a practical gift like a desk accessory or a book about your country. If you receive a business gift and want to reciprocate, give a gift of comparable value, but not more lavish.

In both **Sweden** and **Norway**, alcohol is expensive, so a fine bottle of liquor or wine is a good gift. The most successful gift-giving practice in Norway is to ask your host beforehand if he/she would like you to bring your tax-free quota when flying in. And make sure it is wrapped in quality paper. Gift-giving is not part of the business culture, except for the occasional Christmas present or logo items. And be aware that an excessive gift, or one given before establishing a relationship, can be seen as a bribe.

Ask if you are unsure. On the U.S. Speaker Program to **Belarus**, I wanted to give a gift to the Cultural Attaché in the U.S. Embassy in Minsk who was in charge of my itinerary. I merely asked if they could accept a small gift for the office. I gave them a calendar with beautiful photographic scenes of my home state of Ohio.

Receiving gifts from the Credit Union Association of Belarus.

Sharing photos, maps and cards.

In some cultures, religious beliefs need to be considered when giving gifts. Orthodox **Islam** prohibits images of the human body so do not give pictures of people, and dogs are considered unclean. Avoid gifting silk garments or gold jewelry to men, as both are considered effeminate. Religious concerns also extend to food and beverages. For example, only give vegetarian foods to **Hindus**; only *halal* meat to Orthodox Muslims; and no alcohol, pork, or pigskin products for any Muslims.

If you are giving a gift of food in **Israel**, make sure it is kosher (if the recipient is Orthodox). Also avoid giving gifts until you know the individual better. A book you know they would be interested in makes a good gift. If you are invited to an Israeli home, a simple arrangement of flowers or box of candy is good, and small gifts for the children if they will be there. If it is a holiday, get familiar with the traditional gifts at that time, like honey cakes on Yom Kippur.

In **India** business gifts are not necessary, but if you are invited into an Indian's home you can bring flowers, chocolates, or other gifts that are not readily available in India. When giving money or a check for any occasion, make it an odd number value for good luck (like $101 instead of $100). Do not wrap gifts in white or black, which are unlucky colors, but use bright colors like green, red or yellow. Usually gifts are not opened in the presence of the giver.

In **Morocco**, avoid pink, violet, and yellow, as these are associated with death.

In the **Middle East**, gift-giving is important in the **Arab** countries for generosity and politeness. Arabs will normally be the first to present a gift. Make sure to reciprocate with gifts of similar quality and value whenever possible.

Avoid giving gifts to the wife of an Arab colleague. In fact, do not even inquire about her. Receive gifts with the right hand, never the left. Both hands can be acceptable too. A compass can be a good gift because it can show Muslims the direction of Mecca even when traveling. Also, precious stones, cashmere, crystal or porcelain, and the highest quality of leather (but not pigskin) are considered good gifts.

In an **Egyptian** home, small electronic gadgets, baked goods, or chocolates are a good host/hostess gift, but flowers are only for funerals and weddings.

In **Kuwait**, crafts or picture books from your home region are appreciated, as well as gold pens and business card holders. Remember the male-female protocols, so if a man gives a gift to a female business colleague he should say it is from his female relative.

In **Saudi Arabia**, gifts should be only given to the most intimate of friends. To receive a present from a lesser acquaintance is so embarrassing, it is offensive.

Flowers as a hostess gift are not a good gift from a man, but a woman could give them.

Malaysia is a multicultural, multiethnic society, but follows Muslim guidelines. Business gifts are not exchanged, since they could be seen as a bribe. Even modest inexpensive gift-giving in Malaysia is for friends who have established a personal relationship. However, if you are presented with a gift, accept it with both hands and open it after your colleagues have left. Make sure to reciprocate with a gift of equal value, and offer it with the right hand. Appropriate gifts can be good quality pens, desk accessories, or regional items representing your country or city. A regional food or specialty delicacy is also good. Use red or green wrapping paper, but never white, which symbolizes death. Present the gift shortly before departing.

For the **Chinese in Malaysia**, make sure you give gifts in even numbers, as odd numbers are considered unlucky. And so are the colors white, blue, and black. Stick to wrapping paper in red, pink or yellow. When invited to their home, fruit, sweets, and cakes are good for the host/hostess; you can say it is for the children. Never give clocks; handkerchiefs; flowers, as they are for the sick or at funerals; straw sandals; or anything sharp.

Indians in Malaysia follow Hindu guidelines. Good host/hostess gifts are flowers (never frangipanis flowers, which are only used at funerals) or chocolates wrapped in red, yellow, green, or other brightly colored wrapping paper. Do not give alcohol unless you know the recipient drinks. Only give gifts of money in odd number, and do not give items in multiples of three. Avoid all leather products.

Participation in a local culture and sharing festivities is another kind of gift.

Giving Gifts in China

Many business people are traveling to China nowadays. It is a new frontier. Gift-giving used to be a part of Chinese business etiquette, but with Communism came skepticism, and offering gifts to government officials became illegal. It was considered a form of bribery. Nowadays there is a more relaxed attitude again in the exchange of business gifts in mainland China, but there are no set guidelines.

Although high-end luxury brands (such as Gucci, Dior, and Louis Vuitton) are hard to find in China and well regarded, I suggest you avoid giving any expensive presents to business counterparts. Remember that regional variations exist, so make sure to research the specific region, company, or individual you are visiting ahead of time. Always give your gift with both hands and ceremoniously.

To prevent your business gift from being perceived as a bribe, you can:

- Present the group gifts as your company giving a gift to their company.

- Display your company logo on the gift to make it look like a form of advertising.

- Avoid highly expensive gifts.

Numbers have significant value in Chinese culture and are important to keep in mind when giving a gift. Even numbers are best, except four, which is an unlucky number. (This is also the case in South Korea and Japan.) Gifts in groups of eight bring luck to the recipient, and six is a blessing for smoothness and advancing forward without problems. Eighty-eight and 168 are both lucky numbers and good amounts for money gifts. Single or odd numbers imply loneliness or separation.

Plain red wrapping paper is a safe choice, as red is a lucky color in China. Gold, silver, and pink are also suitable. White, blue, and black carry a negative meaning. And do not give a man a green hat or you will indicate to him his wife is unfaithful. Give the gift with two hands.

Some Things to Keep in Mind

It is a good idea to keep a list of gifts given and received. This will make it easier to write thank you notes and to evaluate a relationship. Make sure you do not duplicate gifts, as it is considered a lack of thoughtfulness. In **China**, do not photograph gift-giving, unless it is a symbolic event. If there are negotiations, wait until they are over before presenting the gift. The most acceptable gift is throwing a banquet.

Keep in mind that in certain languages, some words can have different meanings but be pronounced the same way. In Chinese culture, giving a clock as a gift is taboo because the word "clock" has the same pronunciation as "death." Similarly, in Japan, the word "four" and "death" are homophones, so never give gifts in sets of four.

In **South Korea**, gifts between business associates are a sign of appreciation. Generosity is a good personal trait, so whenever possible, give an expensive gift. There is a dollar amount limit for gifts to civil servants before they have to be reported. It is customary for the receiver of a gift to reciprocate with a gift of similar value at a later date.

In **Taiwan**, do not give a gift that was originally made in Taiwan.

Points to Remember on Giving Gifts

- Research the gift-giving etiquette in the culture/country you are visiting.

- Research the company/individuals you are visiting and think of their interests.

- Gift-giving protocols differ for business and invitations to someone's home.

- If you are meeting in your country, follow your customs. If you are meeting in another country, follow their customs.

- Colors, shapes, and numbers of parts in a gift carry a different meaning in different cultures.

- When receiving an unexpected gift, be aware of the giver's culture to better understand the intention of the gift. Be gracious.

- Consider the value of the gift and whether the culture requires you to reciprocate.

- Politely refuse a gift if it is inappropriate or puts you in an uncomfortable position of obligation.

- Consider when to give a gift. At the beginning or end of a meeting? When you arrive or when you leave?

- Know if you are expected to open the gift in front of the giver or not. Ask if you are not sure.

- Know if you should give your gift in public or private.

- Keep religious beliefs in mind.
- Be aware of gift-giving customs between men and women.
- Keep a list of gifts received and gifts given.
- Your recipient will have to travel with the gift. Avoid heavy or bulky items.

Gifts to Avoid

- Wine from another country or of lesser quality than that produced in the country you are visiting.
- Pigskin products and alcohol to Muslims.
- Leather products to Hindus.
- Leather products in a country that produces high quality leather goods.
- Items you would not want to receive.
- Items that indicate the recipient needs to change, such as a book on self-improvement.
- Gifts that have your company name and logo; they might be perceived as cheap freebies.
- Sharp items such as knives and scissors.
- Items which impose a responsibility on the recipient, like a pet.

Safe Gifts to Give

- Books and DVDs about your home country or city.

- Caps and t-shirts with the name and logo of your home teams for sports enthusiasts.

- Quality desk accessories, pens, business card holders.

- Quality electronic gadgets, calculators.

- Special items that are unique to your country or region, such as Amish cheese, Ohio maple syrup, or Texas chili.

- Disney products for children.

- Gifts that reflect the recipients' tastes and interests.

Points to Remember on Receiving Gifts

- Say "Thank you."

- Try saying "Thank you" in their language.

- If you open it in the front of the giver, always show your pleasure with a smile.

- Take your time to breathe and acknowledge the connection.

The Polite Decline Before the Acceptance

There is an art embedded in receiving a gift. In some cultures, it is more important than in others.

For example, in Japan, everyone politely pretends to refuse once or twice before accepting a gift. It is a kind of ritual that everyone follows. The giver also bows upon offering the gift. And if compliments are given for the gift, no matter how special the gift is, the giver will say it was nothing. Humility reigns.

In China, the custom is to refuse three times while the giver keeps insisting you take it. In Hong Kong, if you accept a gift right away, it is considered greedy.

Even in the U.S., where we are less formal, if the gift is unexpected we might say something like, "Oh, you shouldn't have," or, "I can't accept this" even though you do not literally mean that. Then upon reflection after opening you might say, "You are so generous," or "How kind," or, "How thoughtful," to show appreciation.

OK. Sometimes we just do not know how to reciprocate. A genuine verbal "thank you" may be just enough. In high-context countries where more time is taken to develop relationships, you can reciprocate later and often as you get to know the other person.

Indirect Gifts

Gifts delivered by or offered to a third party can serve as an introduction or to avoid a return obligation or embarrassment for the recipient.

When I delivered gifts from a Russian-American to her friends in St. Petersburg, the presents served as my introduction and connection to their friend in the U.S. I gave them the gifts from me at the end of my visit after I got to know them better and as a thank you for hosting me.

Exchanging flags at Rotary Club in St. Petersburg, Russia.

In 1979, my mother came to visit me in Japan. A group of Japanese private clients invited us to a special dinner. One man wanted to give me a substantial gift, a large Japanese porcelain traditional doll in kimono in a glass case, as a thank you for being his teacher. Because this gift was quite substantial and he did not want to impose a return obligation upon me, he needed to find a way to make it appropriate so there was no mixed message, loss of face, or embarrassment. He turned to my mother, who was the honored guest and said "We hope you enjoyed your visit to Japan. Please accept this souvenir gift and if it is too large to carry back to America, perhaps your daughter would like to keep it for you." The Japanese are indirect, polite, and conscious about protocol.

He used my mother as the decoy for giving me the gift, just as go-betweens are often used in business. Afterwards, my mother said to me, "See the serenity on the Japanese doll's face. Look at it every day, de-stress, and become peaceful."

Group Gift-Giving

There are several ways to handle presents when the whole group is gathered. You can give one group gift that can be shared, such as food items, or one item that can be displayed in the office. You can give one gift to the head person as a gesture for all. Most of the time, you will need to give some kind of gift to each person.

When I was in Belarus, I had a translator for all my presentations to make sure that my rudimentary Russian was not misunderstood. I gave her a gift. There was also the head of the Belarus Coach Federation who had been my initial contact person. At the welcome dinner at her house, I gave a gift to her, her husband, and each of her children. I had researched ahead of time the ages of her children and even asked her what her children might like. At the farewell gathering, I gave a small token gift to other members of the group I had met previously in the U.S. Then, a woman who had been in the background all week gave me a small figurine of Saint Olga, which was also her name. As we were walking out, we held eye contact without words, almost like we didn't want to depart. I reached into my pocket to give her a small something and her face burst into joy. We made a connection for life, and today I still remember her even if we didn't speak the same language.

Do in Rome as the Romans Do

Most importantly, if you are in your own country and giving a gift to a visitor from another culture, follow your own gift-giving custom. This teaches others about your culture. However, remember precautions for men and women and religious sensitivity.

SECTION IV

Points to *Remember* for Specific Countries

Doing Business in Japan

How to Work with Japanese People

Treat them like any other people in the West, but with more formality. Common pitfalls are to talk too much and not listen enough.

Silence could be awkward for you, but the Japanese need time to absorb what is said. If you talk too much, you will not give them space to give you the information you need.

Foreigners also often have trouble understanding when the Japanese disagree. The Japanese are vague, and leave a lot to be read between the lines.

Americans do not leave anything unspoken. Ask specific questions to draw out more information. Follow up if you do not understand what they mean. Do not assume anything.

U.S. culture is very litigious. We use legal documentation more often and with copious details. U.S. contracts are huge, and Japanese contracts are thin.

How to Successfully Work in a Japanese Company as an American

Do not expect to have a clear job description. Even if you have a title, they will not tell you what to do. For the first few weeks they just sit you down with manuals about the company. Look for what you can do and make suggestions.

Japanese bosses expect subordinates to come to them with ideas, instead of them delegating work and telling you what to do. This also creates relationships.

Surviving a Meeting with the Japanese

U.S. meetings have specific goals. There is an agenda and it is easy to take minutes. In the U.S., we get together, put the issues out upfront, brainstorm, decide who is for what, then we are done.

Most Japanese meetings seem purposeless, without agenda, lacking direction, and only scheduled for the sake of having a meeting. If it is set for ninety minutes, it will be exactly ninety minutes. *Nemawashi*, root binding, building relationships by this group activity is the process of making decisions.

In Japan, there are small get-togethers, to get people on board, brainstorm, hash it out, and when they have a meeting, everyone is already in agreement. They are spreading out the process by osmosis. The *nemawashi* process comes from gardening. Each part of the root system gets dug, gets attention.

When you are in a meeting and a decision has to be made, you need to understand psychology. No one wants to stand out as the decision-maker. This is risky, and you could be seen as not part of the team. The best decisions seem to materialize, appearing spontaneous. Japanese do not like surprises. The worst thing is to come unprepared, surprise others, and then have opposition, which they will not verbalize to save you face.

Meetings can be mostly talking in circles, getting comfortable with ideas, and seemingly have no purpose or outcome.

If impatient or frustrated, a Westerner might take over the meeting to move it along. The Japanese might all say, "Yes, yes, we have a deal," but that would not really be the case.

First you have to get to basic agreement. Then you go to the end to final agreement, but then you need another meeting, the post-meeting. Here you meet with a smaller group of people, reconfirm the outcome, and decide who will follow up with what. Sometimes foreigners think they understand the outcome of an agreement, only to realize they have misinterpreted it. So, the post-meeting is important.

Creating Engaged Employees in Japan

With a lot of work in a Japanese company, they do not get a lot of productivity.

Ho-ren-so has three elements: *hokoku, renraku, soudan* meaning reporting, touching base, and discussing. Everyone gets *horenso* training when they first join the company. Sometimes companies require you read their company book by the founder before you even interview.

In New York City at Sony Corporation of America, where I was Manager of Public Relations, I was given the *Sony Vision* book written by Nick Lyons.

In the German and American companies I had worked in, I did not show my work to my boss until it was all done. However, at Nissho Iwai, my Japanese mentor had me do reports on my training, checked in with me regularly and we had discussions each step of the way. A cross-cultural difference for sure.

Japanese are often motivated by fear or to avoid shame. What will others think? Will the boss shout at me? What about my family?

A lot of companies lack progressive discipline in Japan. It is difficult to fire someone. In the U.S., if someone is not performing, they are given a verbal and written warning, a performance improvement plan, and maybe a coach or mentor. If they still have not received the message, they part ways. In Japan, the last step is difficult.

The *shūshin koyō* system is the system of not getting rid of employees or lifetime employment. The company can tell you where to work and for how many hours, and if you do not obey, only then can they fire you. The company owns you…for life.

It is difficult to change jobs. Most Japanese cannot survive in the labor market. They can put together a resume, survive an interview, but do not know where they fit into the market. Therefore, headhunters are the norm in Japan today.

Japanese Management Culture

In 1933, Konosuke Matsushita created seven guiding principles, renamed the "Seven Spirits of Matsushita" in his honor. Matsushita firmly believed that a business as large as his was responsible to help all of society prosper. They are an extension of the Japanese culture into business and still used today at Matsushita Electric and other Japanese companies.

- Service through industry
- Fairness and honesty
- Harmony and cooperation
- Struggle for progress
- Courtesy and humility
- Adjustment and assimilation
- Gratitude

More Elements of Japanese Business Culture

- *Giri:* The sense of duty or obligation is ingrained in the culture. It can also become a burden. *Giri* is less important in the newer generations.

- The sense of *giri* can be seen in how Japan has the lowest rate of laying off employees. Employees often return the loyalty by only consuming products made by the company they work for.

- *Senpai* and *kōhai*: *Senpai* is someone of a higher age or senior level, who coaches the *kōhai*, a junior. This mentoring system is found in all levels of education, organizations, sports and business. It is an essential element of Japanese seniority-based status relationships with reciprocal obligations.

Introducing a New Product in Japan

It is not easy to introduce a product or service into another culture. Many businesses fail when they try to expand globally.

You need to consider how much to adapt to the new culture to be a success. Something new can be attractive, but on the other hand, the culture needs to be open to new ideas and the product or service needs to fit into its lifestyle.

Trying to adapt too much and not adapting enough can bring failure.

Starbucks is a great success story. In 1996, they opened their first location outside the U.S. in Tokyo. Now it is the biggest coffee chain in Japan, with a market share of forty-eight percent. The secret of their success may lie in the balance between maintaining the trendiness of being an American brand and adapting to the Japanese market.

As for innovation, the nonsmoking environment appealed to the younger generation, drive-throughs were added in the suburban areas, and Kindle tablets are now available in the foreign business-district coffee shops in Tokyo.

Starbucks also took steps to become familiar with Japanese culture. Japanese value the top quality customer service. Concept stores were specifically designed to complement the atmosphere of certain neighborhoods. The Japanese love tradition and national festivals, so seasonal drinks such as *Sakura* (Cherry Blossom) Frappuccino are offered. They are also very private, so Starbucks removed its signature service of writing down the customer's name with their order.

Many businesses fail to understand the extent a culture values tradition. Cultural norms are deeply held in the psychology and social history of a people. To be successful, you need to look beyond the exterior of urban trends and modernization.

There is an initial boom for many companies, but sustaining it is another matter.

Doing Business in Belarus and Russia

Belarussians use a people-to-people approach. How a person behaves, looks, speaks, dresses, and so on are important.

When I was speaking and presenting in Belarus, I dressed in my professional suit attire with comfortable traditional black heels. Fashionable leather footwear is popular in Belarus, and it turned out my shoes were not trendy enough. My translator, Iryna, took me to the underground shopping area and suggested I could get a pair of boots or shoes along with my other more typical Belarussian-made purchases. I chose a pair of ankle-high heel boots with a cuff and she exclaimed how much better they looked.

During the next day as we went from presentation to presentation, she drew others attention to my new boots several times. "Look how nice her new footwear is." It seems I needed to up my game in the shoe department to be seen as a complete package presenter.

Business meetings in Belarus are to present and collect questions. More often participants are silent. Belarussians make decisions after the meetings. With government and state officials, everyone looks at what the leader does.

For the younger generation, thirty-five and under, they may make their own decisions, are more open-minded, and speak out. It depends on the industry.

Coach University with Belarusian Trainers, and my boots.

Trust is necessary with Belarussians. In business, they check documents and contracts, history and figures, recommendations, and performance results.

One Do, One Don't for Americans Visiting Belarus or Russia

Do speak to people, be friendly, and try to participate in community activities.

Don't try to show you are bigger than you are. They see success as more concrete with proven results from projects in the past.

After my draniki *(potato pancake) welcome party in Minsk, the group wishes me good night.*

Doing Business in China

In the Chinese business environment, complimenting and rewarding employees is not usually done publically. Subordinates defer to their seniors. Mentors and executives may display a paternalistic concern toward their juniors. As you go higher up the ranks in large Chinese businesses and organizations, you are also going higher up in the government bureaucracy, and projects and negotiations can change from the immediate goals. Be patient. They need to deal with a chain of command.

Patience is key. The Chinese bargain well. They approach negotiating as a win-lose scenario. They might come on as the poor Chinese, and you are the powerful rich Westerner, which puts you in the position of the teacher expected to provide everything for the student. They use many negotiating tricks, giving up what is not valuable to them and expecting you to give up something valuable in return, or stalling and delaying until you are almost ready to leave China.

The Chinese are tough negotiators.

Tips for the American include: stay with win-win negotiating strategies based on equal relationships, and remember that to the Chinese, a contract is merely a piece of paper signifying the beginning of a business relationship. Things can change over time. Stay in touch, share more information than you expect, and have a contact in China who can keep you informed.

A Comparison of Different Customs for Introductions

In **Japan**, a formal introduction is the best way to get your foot in the door and establish a business relationship. Some degree of connection is useful (for example if you went to the same university or are part of the same organization).

In **Arab** countries, introductions are not necessary. You don't need an introduction to get your foot in the door. You can introduce yourself, based on your own merit. But do not mistake it. They are definitely a more relational than transactional culture.

In the **U.S.** an introduction holds a more potential business outcome, but introductions are not required. We network and lead people to each other, but we do not take responsibility for how they relate to each other afterwards. We are more transactional, not relational. Cold-calling and mass marketing are common. The product and price are what sell, not necessarily how you got to the prospective buyer.

In comparison, getting an introduction in **China** is most important. It protects you.

It is common practice and easier to get than you think. The introducer has incentive because they gain exposure and also a favor in return. As long as you can pay for it, you do not need to know someone personally for them to introduce you.

Elements of Chinese Business Culture

After the introduction, make a verbal agreement. When you start to agree, there is a kind of ceremonial formality that follows. You may find yourself eating together banquet-style and toasting in honor of the new relationship. (See Lesson 12: Entertaining, Etiquette, and Seating.) This shows there is a contractual future.

Keep in mind this Chinese business saying: "He who forgets favors is not loyal."

Here are some cultural foundations of Chinese business:

- *Guanxi*: The network of personal contacts, not necessarily experience and education, is a Chinese executive's most important asset.

- *Zhongjian Ren*: The use of an intermediary to make introductions and resolve differences is important.

- *Shehui Dengji*: The hierarchy is acknowledged. Only second-level executives, the hard negotiators, show opposition and enter discussions on important topics, never the highest-ranking executives.

- *Renji Hexie*: Harmonious relationships are important. Take time to build mutual trust and friendship before doing business.

- *Zhengti Guannian*: There is a more global, expansive, holistic focus in business topics. Do not negotiate step-by-step in a sequential way. This can cause delays and become frustrating. Be patient.

- *Jie Jian:* A frugal society, they have extreme negotiation and aggressive bargaining tactics. They hit extremely low prices—lower than they are realistically willing to accept—as a tactic to weaken their counterpart.

- *Mianzi*: Reputation is important. Actions that can result in losing face, such as interrupting someone, directly challenging someone, or pointing out someone's error should be avoided.

- *Gei Mianzi*: Giving face with compliments and praising someone's work in front of a superior is good.

- *Chiku Nailao*: Persistence and resistance show hard work is valued over talent and creativity. They are patient and delay making final decisions as a pressure strategy.

- *Lunlixue*: Ethics are different than in the West. They change conditions previously agreed upon. Have a good intermediary, and take into account cultural elements such as reputation, hierarchy and harmony.

Morality is based on the circumstances of the moment and not on universal principles, according to Confucius.

Doing Business in Fenno-Scandinavia

In the U.S., we are very concerned with risk management, and have copious written agreements. But, in Finland, when they agree, it is with a handshake and a few words.

This applies to all Nordic countries, with some cultural differences between these countries.

Americans see Europe as one market, but it is not. Consider if the U.S. company in Fenno-Scandinavia has roots in Europe or in the U.S. There is an internal difference.

Finns are a transactional culture. They are reserved and efficient. They do not talk much. When they decide, they implement.

The Swedes discuss business issues over and over to be sure everyone is on the same page, but not as much as in South America or Japan.

At the dinner table in Helsinki, Finland with a group of friends, I was the only non-Finn. Everyone spoke to me in English and everyone spoke in English to each other because I was there. At one point, there were two people speaking to each other in Finnish but as soon as I passed them a plate or looked their way they switched to English.

English speakers visiting Nordic countries find it very easy to communicate. The school system emphasizes learning the English language (British English). In general, training materials for even blue collar workers can be in English.

A Comparison of Different Conversational Styles

I was invited by Kyrgyz colleagues to join a tour they organized for a group of Finns. After hours on the bus, I tried to converse with some of the Finnish passengers. At one point, a woman named Tina said, "We do not do small talk." She was letting me know not to take it personally if the conversations tended to be short or not as elaborately engaging. This was reaffirmed for me in Finland too.

In Spain and Italy, people will easily talk at the same time or interject comments without pausing to wait for the other to finish. They will also speak for a longer period of time.

In the U.S. and Northern Europe, one person will speak at a time and for a shorter duration than in Latin countries. But, if there is an increase in emotion, a disagreement, or a question, they will interrupt.

In Japan, the pauses between phrases and the pauses between speakers is at the other extreme. They will speak for a shorter period of time, then pause or wait for someone else to speak before commenting again.

Naturally, we must allow for individual personality difference within each culture as well.

Business in Fenno-Scandinavia

Mikael, a Finnish executive commented on planning and design. "When the task is given, the Americans act. But the group ending the task is the Japanese."

Here are his comparisons between the Americans and the Finns in business:

- Finns are more relational in business.
- Finns use the best person for the job.
- Finns find small talk a killer.

- Finns see Americans as results-oriented and competitive. Even the laid-back Californian is considered extremely competitive.

- Finns in business have a very high engineering talent.

- Looking at three areas of business customer intimacy, process efficiency, and product expertise, Finns are best in product expertise.

In Finland and Sweden, the telecommunications companies Nokia and Ericsson were booming at the same time and the processes can be seen cross-culturally.

The Swedes look at what they will be doing. They launch the product, new models, and create hype months ahead of time. They are good at marketing.

The Finns are more humble. They look at what they have done and tell about it afterwards. They have a new model and when it is launched, they say "It will be in the shops tomorrow." They're not strong at marketing.

SECTION V

Noble *Directions* for Global Connections

The Compass Within

"It is not our purpose to become each other; it is to recognize each other, to learn to see the other and honor him for what he is."

— HERMANN HESSE

My personal story illustrates my American culture and upbringing and how it overlaps with cross-cultural considerations: individualism, internal control and belief in change, innovation and comfort with risk, the entrepreneurial spirit, and try-try-try again. They are the foundation for how I took actions to move through my life.

However, from my world travels, I have also embraced the culture of formality, respect for elders, and an admiration for history and tradition in ancient practices that have survived the ages. Who I was before, and who I have become, shows me the interplay of fate and personal control.

I have changed through cross-cultural experiences. But the foundation of that change was probably already in my personality and psyche—and being from a culture where I am allowed to be independent, innovative, and to embrace change. So they work together.

I do not believe my actions and thoughts are isolated from others'. If I am questioning or comparing myself with concepts like, "what is the norm?", "what do others think?" or "what have others done?", then I am not attuning to my personal path. This creates an internal stress, which disallows that which is personally right for me.

When I feel good inside, when I am doing what feels right for me, I know I am attracting that which best supports me, and I will in turn affect others with that positivity and flow.

The steps it took to get here are simple, yet profound.

Three Cross-Cultural Directions for Successful Overseas Business

1. Awareness of similarities and differences

2. Acceptance of their existence

3. Adjustment in business strategies

First, be aware: aware of yourself and your inner dialogue, and aware of what you see in others.

Secondly, from this awareness, do everything in your power to move into acceptance. Accept what you see of yourself and accept what you see in others without comparison, judgment, analyzing, or wishing it were different.

Overcoming resistance to anything, let alone opposing cultural practices, is not always easy. However, it will not only help you with building lasting business relationships, but also impact other areas of your life.

Thirdly, this will lead to adjustment—within yourself. This shift moves you to more deeply connect with your intuitive creative self and with the hearts of others. Then adjustment in the other may happen.

Direction 1: Awareness

Having a deep awareness of yourself can show how you respond to life's ups and downs. This in turn helps you have an awareness of others. Knowing how your culture influences the way you do business makes it easier to be aware of other cultures' business practices. Then you become empowered to do business with ease overseas.

Body-mind techniques are a great way to become more aware of stress. One of my favorites is meditative yoga. When you quiet the mind, you become more aware of the body's areas of tension. You get in touch with your inner self.

The mind compares, analyzes, judges, and interprets life. It stays in our past perceptions or jumps to our future expectations. It is attached to desire.

The body, however, lives in the present moment. When we focus the mind on body sensations and the breath, the body-mind connection creates another dimension, a sense of well-being which opens the heart.

Awareness brings relaxation.

Direction 2: Acceptance

You cannot accept something unless you are aware of it.

Resistance is an attachment to holding on to what you have, or pushing away what you do not want. You can actually notice the tension either way in your body.

Relaxing the body affects the mind. Allowing the judgmental mind to relax helps you to let go into infinite possibilities.

When you relax, you are more open to see people and situations as they are.

Accepting yourself for who you are right now, without trying to make anything different, allows you to let go of the stress of trying to be someone else. Knowing and accepting yourself as you are gives you the compassion and understanding to accept others as they are.

In intercultural relations, you come face-to-face with people from countries with different ways of doing business. Being able to accept these differences—to bridge the gap—is crucial to succeed.

Accepting life's experiences, no matter how they manifest, is the key to making conscious choices to change.

Direction 3: Adjustment

Adjustment of how you view yourself, others, and life's experiences can only come after acceptance of what really is. Otherwise, any adjustment will only be temporary.

In business, this means adjusting to another culture's business practice, compromising and accommodating where possible. This demonstrates awareness and respect.

Change, real change, comes from within.

You cannot *think* yourself to enlightenment. You need to *feel* it.

Observe the thinking mind as if you were a witness to it, watching it without reaction. Then you will connect to your core, to a state of being beyond the mind.

Adjusting to people and situations can be stressful. Stress will lead you into reaction, a reacting from old patterns of thought and behavior. You are in your thinking mind with filtered memories of what was, and perceptions of what will come. However, if you are at ease, you respond instead of react. You move from thinking and doing, to being and feeling. You access a conscious state of mind based in love, moving into the heart. You become connected to yourself, others, and the whole of life itself.

Awareness
Acceptance
Adjustment

Three As

The Three *As* Applied

> ## "Do everything with so much love in your heart that you would never want to do it any other way."
> ### — YOGI AMRIT DESAI

While in the Dominican Republic, the mode of transport to the outskirts of the capital to get to the villages and remote parts of the country was an open-back pick-up truck. As I waited on a folding chair on the roadside, the truck came by and we stepped up. I became aware of my situation. I knew Spanish and I heard people mutter or even shout phrases which meant "It's too full. You are crowding me in." But as a hand reached to help me up, a small spot opened up. We were accepted.

As we rode, the spot became larger and the crowd shifted to accommodate us, the newest passengers. There was an adjustment. Bumping along, our bodies touched, a few squeals came out, and pretty soon people were joking and smiling.

Then we stopped again. More people wanted in. As they hopped on, the crowd was now grumbling and resisting again. Interestingly, I was now part of the established group, no longer the newcomer. And the shift happened again; they were incorporated and accepted into the group and along the way we all became one—until the next stop.

The cycle continued over and over. Awareness of a resistance, then acceptance, followed by adjustment.

Business Ease Overseas: Building Cross-Cultural Relationships That Last

Relax and De-Stress

Creativity flows more easily when we are relaxed. When we are under stress, we move out of our gut feeling and into a mindset in which actions are determined by trying to avoid something, or fear of failure. This also applies when we do business overseas. Relaxing makes us more flexible to take it a moment at a time, have patience, courage, and keep trying. The best resolution will come as we get more experienced.

Have a Positive Attitude

With a positive outlook, you get your foot in the door and are on your way to building relationships that last. Focus on successes. Use affirming language. The law of attraction brings more. When you are positive, you see your cup as half full and not half empty. Then you actually have a shift energetically that attracts more of the same.

Ask for Help, Have Mentors, and Help Others

We do not live in isolation. Building relationships that last requires human interchange and sharing of ourselves. Use the insights of diverse staff and consultants to connect with diverse customers and new markets.

Observe and Know Yourself

Know yourself, your own cultural thoughts and behaviors, and the ways in which these may influence how you do business.

Respect Differences

Be observant of others. Be nonjudgmental. See differences not as dividing points, but as the building blocks of platforms for innovation and moving forward.

Respect differences with the Three *As*: Awareness, Acceptance, and Adjustment. Your adjustment may be a shift inside yourself to become comfortable in a situation, or a shift in your normal behavior. It could be as simple as different ways of time management. Or, it could be a transformational experience for you. It can broaden your perspectives and forge new avenues for making relationships happen, work, and continue.

Be in the Moment and Be Flexible

Be open to unexpected situations. If you do not resist change, you can embrace and learn from it. If you resist changes which cannot be helped, you waste time and energy. Change your mindset. Then you can see what really *is*. If you see the present situation clearly, you see how it affects the future at the same time.

Go off the Beaten Path and Be Fearless

New people to meet, new opportunities to find. Some of the most unexpected events become the best stories to tell when you return home.

Be Authentic and Find Your Uniqueness

Connect naturally in your own way. Be true to yourself. Embrace the uniqueness in yourself and discover it as well in others.

See the Bigger Picture and Focus on Commonalities

Take time to learn a few greetings in their language ("Hello" and "Thank you").

Eat some local dishes. Interact with the public. People want to do business with people they know, like and trust. Find common areas of interest. Focus on the similarities. See the bigger picture. Then the differences will be less overwhelming.

Recognize Collective Consciousness

We all have a role, large or small, in what is happening in our world. Our thoughts and choices are a part of a collective consciousness.

If we are fearful and stressed, we start to think negatively. We spiral downward instead of upward. Our energy shifts and negatively affects others.

If we are peaceful inside, we align with who we really are, to our Source, beyond our minds. This uplifts others we come in contact with. We think more clearly and can make conscious choices for action.

AFTERWORD

For Your Continued Journey, Inside and Out

> "In the stillness of the quiet, if we listen, we can hear the whisper of the heart giving strength to weakness, courage to fear, hope to despair."
> —Howard Thurman

As with anything new, you start with will-power and a guide or structure to follow. You search for information, follow the rules, and expect the promised results. You think. You act.

When the unknown becomes more known, you are more comfortable. You are more creative to explore, experiment, and personalize your experience. You see. You let go.

Finally, when you are at ease, you find your intuition comes to the forefront. You look beyond the information to your inner guide. You feel. You know.

The informative parts of this book are meant to be your external guide. The stories are meant to encourage you to have experiences of your own. The positive attitude is meant to shine a light so that you can find and trust your own way.

Just take time to recognize and give thanks for what you have. Sit quietly. Breathe in. Breathe out.

As you move deeper into the stillness, watch your thoughts as if they are on a movie screen passing by. Witness without reaction. Relax.

From this quiet place, you will discover your path to make a difference. You help create a world that works. Small or large steps, every thought and feeling contributes to the collective consciousness.

Choose love.

The future is in all our hands.

Enjoy the journey.

ACKNOWLEDGMENTS

All who have touched my life for brief moments or endless years have helped me see myself more clearly. For all experiences and interactions, the pleasant and the challenging, I am grateful. Without them, I would not be who I am in this moment, in this book, in this way.

The first teachers in life are our parents. I am grateful for my mother, Melva Galatha Russell, who on Earth and now in spirit supported me to follow my dreams, spread my wings, and fly.

I am grateful for my father, Anson Henry Russell. I can count on him, ask him questions, and hear his stories. Inspired by reading his thesis about traveling up the Yangtze River as a young man in the Navy in 1946, I am glad I can share this book with him in his ninetieth year.

I appreciate my teachers of language and life, specifically Spanish Professor Nancy Lopez-Balboa, for opening my eyes to another culture with her stories of Cuba; Reiji Nagakawa, Japanese sensei, for introducing me to the high adventure of traveling Marco Polo's Silk Route; and Professor Marina Kurkov, for her dedication to teaching me Russian. I am grateful to Yogi Amrit Desai (Gurudev) for his guidance over the past thirty years and his transformative teachings of yoga as a journey of self-discovery through the interplay of body, mind, and heart.

For the development of this book, I thank: Jessica

McKeown, who listened to my stories in its preconception phase; Oda-Karoline Rosland Eilertsen, my Norwegian student, who read and edited the initial manuscript; and specific-country business resources—Mikael Vuompo (Finland); Matt Koren (China); Angela O'Connor (Middle-East); Margarita Korzoun (Belarus); Federico Macias-Baena (Spain); and Nita Singh (India); among other associates and clients from whom I have learned in my cross-cultural trainings and business consulting work.

For the actual production of this book, I thank Indie Books International and their team network: Mark LeBlanc, Growing Your Business coach, for his words "extreme focus," which kept on and on in my head; Henry DeVries, for his developmental coaching, marketing knowledge and humor; Devin DeVries, for overseeing operations; Kim Story for his editorial input and first read-through; Denise Montgomery, for her copyediting and taking time to answer my copious questions on linguistic details; and Joni McPherson, for design and graphics.

I appreciate my personal friend, Laighne Fanney, who helped me reframe my thinking to the highest positive vibration on our regular coaching calls.

Most of all, I cannot express in words how grateful I am for my husband, Anthony DeCola, and his constant support. He was with me each step of the way, contributing his unique perspectives, and bringing me homemade chai each morning to keep me going. His daily presence in my life is a steady source of comfort and love.